GU00738206

ABOUT THE AUTHOR

John Higgins is the first Chief Executive of the Western Development Partnership Board, Sligo. He was the first General Manager of IRD Kiltimagh Limited, the community development company that, in the period 1990 to 1994, put Kiltimagh back on its feet.

Born in Ballyhaunis, Co Mayo, where he still lives, John is a teacher by profession and holds a BA in Economics and the Certified Diploma in Accounting and Finance.

John's interest in community development affairs spans over twenty years — he was nominated Ballyhaunis Person of the Year in 1976 for voluntary community endeavour.

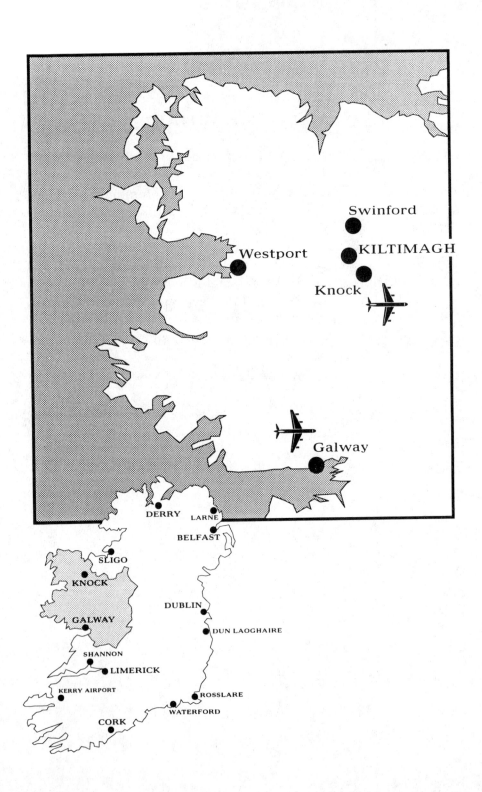

The Kiltimagh Renewal

Best Practice in Community Enterprise

JOHN HIGGINS

Oak Tree Press

Dublin

Oak Tree Press
Merrion Building
Lower Merrion Street
Dublin 2

© 1996 John Higgins
Cover design by Denise Cusack
IRD Kiltimagh logo designed by Tom Meenaghan

A catalogue record is available for this book
from the British Library.

ISBN 1-86076-011-2

All rights reserved. No part of this publication may
be reproduced or transmitted in any form or by any
means, including photocopying and recording,
without written permission of the publisher. Such
written permission must also be obtained before
any part of this publication is stored in a retrieval
system of any nature. Requests for permission
should be directed to Oak Tree Press,
Merrion Building, Lower Merrion Street,
Dublin 2, Ireland.

Printed in Ireland by Colour Books Ltd.

Contents

Section 3:
A Philosophy of Community Enterprise

Appendices

Acknowledging a Team Effort

Vital to the success of any enterprise is the calibre of the team involved. In Kiltimagh, I received the support of many committed people to whom I shall always be grateful.

Working Groups

The following were team members of the many Working Groups that played a vital role in implementing the IRD Kiltimagh Programme:

- ◊ Paul Brennan
- ◊ Monica Browne
- ◊ Anne Marie Carroll
- ◊ Rita Carroll
- ◊ Mona Dempsey
- ◊ Don Dillon
- ◊ Pat Dillon
- ◊ Danny Doherty
- ◊ Carmel Dooley
- ◊ Margaret Freeman
- ◊ Chris Glynn
- ◊ Geraldine Glynn
- ◊ Frank Herraghty
- ◊ Tom Higgins
- ◊ Eugene Ivers
- ◊ Brendan Killeen
- ◊ Gerry King
- ◊ Henry King
- ◊ Michael Laffey
- ◊ Nancy Lavin

◊   Michael Mahoney
◊   Michael Munnelly
◊   Aiden McDonagh
◊   Adrian McHugh
◊   Kieran McHugh
◊   Ann McNicholas
◊   Anthony McNicholas
◊   Brenda McNicholas
◊   Francis McNicholas
◊   Thomas McNicholas
◊   Michael O'Sullivan
◊   Paul O'Shea
◊   Nancy Shannon
◊   Frances Spindler
◊   Kathleen Tarpey
◊   Anne Walsh
◊   Joe Young

Professional Team

The professional team consisted of:

◊   Virginia Brennan
◊   Aisling Cahill
◊   Bernie Connell
◊   Claire Cunnane
◊   Anne Devine
◊   Mary Glynn
◊   Joe Kelly
◊   Tommy Leonard
◊   Bridie McMahon
◊   Mary Nolan
◊   Anna Maria Stuart
◊   Joan Tarpey

The Mentors

Valuable advice and guidance for the Kiltimagh Development Team came from the cross-sector Board of Directors. The following served, or continue to serve, as members of the Board of IRD Kiltimagh Limited:

- Local Community Representatives:

  ◊ Brian Mooney, Coorahoor, Kiltimagh — Chairman since 1989
  ◊ Patricia Dillon, Cordarragh, Kiltimagh
  ◊ Pat English, Killeadan, Kiltimagh
  ◊ Francis McNicholas, Cordarragh, Kiltimagh
  ◊ Nancy Lavin, Derrykinlough, Kiltimagh
  ◊ Sadie Mulhern, Main Street, Kiltimagh — Financial Controller since 1991
  ◊ Thomas McNicholas, Cordarragh, Kiltimagh
  ◊ Christopher Glynn, James Street, Kiltimagh
  ◊ Aiden McDonagh, Killeadan, Kiltimagh
  ◊ Brendan Killeen, Cloondoulough, Kiltimagh
  ◊ Charles Gilmartin, Main Street, Kiltimagh
  ◊ Brenda McNicholas, Cordarragh, Kiltimagh — Secretary since 1993
  ◊ Patrick McNicholas, Main Street, Kiltimagh (Retired)
  ◊ Larry McEllin, Greyfield, Kiltimagh (Retired)
  ◊ Michael Farrington, Park Road, Kiltimagh (Retired)
  ◊ Sean Conway, Cloonkedagh, Kiltimagh (Retired)
  ◊ Pat Costello, Main Street, Kiltimagh (Retired)
  ◊ Padraic Brennan, Cordarragh, Kiltimagh (Retired)
  ◊ Anne Marie Carroll, Park Road, Kiltimagh (Retired) — Secretary 1989–93
  ◊ Jarlath Heneghan, Gortgarve, Kiltimagh (Retired) — Financial Controller 1989–91.

- State Agencies and Local Authority Representatives:

  ◊ Sean Smyth, County Development Officer, Castlebar, replaced by Frank Fullard, CEO, Mayo County Enterprise Board
  ◊ Tom Hyland, IDA Galway, replaced by Mr Billy Walsh, Forbairt, Galway
  ◊ Brian Quinn, Mayo Senior Tourism Officer, Westport
  ◊ Terry Gallagher, CAO, Teagasc, Castlebar
  ◊ Ann McGovern, Director, External Training, FÁS, Galway
  ◊ Vincent Roache, North Western Regional Fisheries Manager, Ballina (Retired).

- Private-Sector Representatives:

  ◊ Philip Mullally, Chief Executive, Enterprise Trust, Dublin
  ◊ Pat O'Connor, Solicitor, Swinford
  ◊ Tom Byrne, J & D Davy, Stockbrokers, Dublin (Retired).

The Supporters

Supporters are invaluable to any team. The supporters of the IRD Kiltimagh Team are too numerous to mention individually. Special mention must go, however, to the good people of Kiltimagh who provided the funding to support the development process. Then there are the many sponsors of projects, the state agency and local authority staff, the civil service, our politicians and the many areas of the media that took particular interest in the IRD Kiltimagh story.

Support also came from former natives of Kiltimagh and associates in many parts of Ireland and overseas — in particular:

- The "Friends of Kiltimagh", Dublin:
  - ◊ Tom Byrne
  - ◊ Tom Jordan
  - ◊ Vinnie Kilduff
  - ◊ Francis Meenaghan
  - ◊ Tom Meenaghan
  - ◊ James Morrissey
  - ◊ John Ronayne
  - ◊ Frank Walsh.

- The "Friends of Kiltimagh", London:
  - ◊ Tom Biesty
  - ◊ Monica (Carroll) Browne
  - ◊ Helen Carroll.

- The "Friends of Kiltimagh", Manchester:
  - ◊ Michael Forde
  - ◊ Pius Forde.

- The "Friends of Kiltimagh", USA:
  - ◊ Chris Benson
  - ◊ Liam Benson
  - ◊ Mike Cummings
  - ◊ Tom Flatley
  - ◊ Paul McGonigle
  - ◊ Paul O'Dwyer
  - ◊ Joe O'Leary
  - ◊ Padraig Walsh
  - ◊ Joseph Walsh.

Foreword

All involved with IRD Kiltimagh in the past five years, together with the hundreds of people in Ireland and overseas who supported our efforts, will no doubt feel a great sense of satisfaction at the development and achievement chronicled in this scholarly and well-researched book. However, on reflection, this satisfaction will probably be tinged with a little sadness that this once thriving market town with its industries and commercial activity could have declined to a level where such dramatic remedial intervention was required.

In the 1980s, the decay brought about by emigration, national isolation and the resulting changes in the fabric of rural society was very evident in Kiltimagh and other towns across Ireland. This scenario had been foreseen by John Healy, a Mayo-born journalist based in Dublin, in his book, *Death of an Irish Town*, written in the 1960s. When no official response was forthcoming, slowly the realisation dawned that initiative would have to come from within the community.

The willingness of Kiltimagh people to co-operate had long manifested itself in the cultural, sporting, charitable and community organisations which continued to prosper despite adversity. But it was the stark results of a survey — showing that 90 out of every 100 children leaving our school were leaving the area — that provided the stimulus which resulted in the formation of IRD Kiltimagh, of which John Higgins was the first General Manager.

The analytical skills and professional approach that John applied to the compilation of this book were the hallmark of his tenure in that position. His commitment to the realisation of the ideas and aspirations of IRD Kiltimagh, the voluntary group that employed him, was complete. He harnessed fully the voluntary effort for which Kiltimagh is legendary, as well as gaining support from a wide network of local people, now resident in England and the USA.

If any lesson can be learnt from reading this book, I hope it will be the importance of marrying community endeavour and goodwill with professional expertise to attain realistic goals which can enhance the lives of the people at all levels.

We still have much to achieve but we go forward with optimism on the evidence of this book. John Higgins can justifiably do likewise.

Brian Mooney
Chairman, IRD Kiltimagh

Preface

The need to redefine the concept of "local" when applied to a system of public administration is now more evident than ever as individuals and communities become restless to bring about a change in the environment in which they live. There is a greater realisation that self-reliance and self-help are the only answer to stimulating enterprising communities from which will spring the salvation of our national economy.

In the past, individuals and communities were complacent in believing that someone "up there" would do it for us. Our religious beliefs and our history had led us to rely on a higher power. At local level, the better-educated members of the community — the priest and the school teacher — were looked to for the solution to local problems. The current emphasis on global economics has led to the neglect of local economies, and eventually the realisation has dawned that no one was "doing it for us".

The Kiltimagh Renewal: Best Practice in Community Enterprise was written to stimulate the process of local re-awakening. While lip-service is paid to the concepts of subsidiarity and regionalisation, there is no real political commitment in our country, or in Europe generally, towards either process. Within a well-educated Europe, why can't individuals and communities be allowed to decide their own destiny, to administer their own systems and to provide tradable goods and services in a free market to their neighbouring communities?

This book was written from my experiences in Kiltimagh, County Mayo — a community where real jobs and real economic development have been fostered in a few short years. Its success story is relative in that it can only be judged against what other communities have not yet decided to do. Kiltimagh decided to adopt a self-help approach to solving its local problems. In doing so, it relied for assistance in the first instance not on state systems but on its own resources, both financial and human, and on the resources of the private business sector by way of advice and assistance from the IRD Trust (now the Enterprise Trust).

Kiltimagh, like many other towns in Ireland, expanded as a small market centre in the early to mid-nineteenth century. These towns were centres where craftsmen located and business was transacted between the rural population and their urban neighbours, as the new commercial order grew because of the greater interdependence of monetary trading systems. Such towns were to witness peaks and troughs of development. In particular, the small towns of the West of Ireland witnessed some very severe depressions — including the disastrous famine of 1847–49, which swept millions of people off the small farms of Ireland. These depressions deprived the market towns of much-needed rural population, on which the economic order of Irish towns could be built.

Ironically, it was 100 years later, in the 1940s and 1950s, that these towns were once again hit by a silent, but equally deadly, plague — massive forced emigration of people from rural areas in search of much-needed work opportunities presented by the post-war building boom in Britain. This emigration trail, which for the previous 100 years had been focused mainly on transatlantic migration to the great new world of the United States, was now directed eastwards. The Irish phenomenon of seasonal movements began: after the summer's work was completed on the small farms of the West of Ireland, the winter job was again resumed in Britain in order to allow the family members to be reared in the "safety" of Ireland. And so it was that the "Culchie", as the Kiltimagh native has come to be called, came to be found on the building sites of Britain.

In the mid-1970s and 1980s, crisis time came once again for the small towns of rural Ireland. The difference in our generation is that the emigration trail, which was difficult in the mid-1800s, is now more easily accessible. England is near at hand, allowing regular visits home to see loved ones. The "pull" of relatives in exile is also present. More deadly still, however, is that the "push" from the homeland continues to exert pressure to emigrate.

My purpose in writing this book is to examine the unavoidable aspects of this "push" of emigration, to try to focus on our mistakes and, more importantly, to learn from them. I hope that, by sounding the SOS, villages and communities in Ireland may be stimulated to respond. Communities and small businesses must think positively and respond to changing market forces and to new opportunities. The "emergency and rescue" services which have the power to change our lives by political decisions, acting through the arms of state, must react practically and positively to support local communities in responding to the crisis.

Failure to realise that small changes make big differences in the local economic order is one of the great obstacles. The gap between the "bottom-up" (community) approach to development and the more firmly established "top-down" approach must be filled. A new dynamic must be established in the "centre", if enterprise is to flourish in Ireland.

President Robinson's "silent revolution" is the new approach to development which communities are determined to undertake, in the realisation that "self-help" is the only tonic that can cure economic decay. In the words of the Progressive Democrats' leader, Mary Harney, "If job creation agencies and reports on unemployment were the way to solve the crisis, Ireland would have full employment".

Our country must rid itself of the curse of centralisation. Too much control is vested in central government. This leads to the reliance on global economics, and to a tragic reneging by the state on the provision of appropriate support systems to enhance local economic sustainment by reducing dependency on grants and subsidies.

Unfortunately, the signs are that we have learned little from the mistakes of the past. The present system of dispensing the second round of Structural Funds is proceeding along the same path of "throwing money" at the problem from on high. In doing this, the state is determined, rightly, to ensure that public money is not wasted. But there is too much emphasis on avoiding wastage and too little emphasis on the effect of public spending, which I contend is so diluted by bureaucracy that the return on investment is minimal.

This book is divided into three sections, outlining important phases and events of my work as a community development manager. *Section 1* provides the background and gives an account of my experiences while working at the pit-face of community enterprise. During the five-year period from 1990 to 1994, the Kiltimagh community undertook a mammoth development programme which is described in detail in the case study in *Section 2*. In *Section 3*, I present my personal philosophy of community enterprise in order to provide assistance to other local community associations trying to plan their own community programmes.

This sharing of my experiences is an effort to bring about a debate to ensure that this failed process of development is halted, to ask for an immediate rethink and to encourage community leaders and private business to work together to overcome the serious obstacles that exist. The success story of Kiltimagh's fight for economic survival should encourage all of us to continue trying.

John Higgins
Sligo
December 1995

1
Introduction

The determination to bring about a change in the local economic malaise that had beset Kiltimagh led to the establishment of a development company, IRD Kiltimagh Limited, in 1989.

This company mobilised the local people who, with the help of emigrants overseas, raised £111,000 in subscriptions in a four-year period — no mean achievement for a population base of 2,500. The principle of "Kiltimagh Economics" was to amass a significant local (core) fund and to seek to create a large multiplier effect from the various state assistance programmes. The actual multiplier effect was in the ratio of 7:1 — far in excess of what had been anticipated.

The decision by the local community to employ a full-time manager (myself) to achieve its goals was in itself a landmark, the idea being to combine local funds and professional management so as to stimulate local enterprise. In all of this, support for the enterprise process came from the private business sector, in particular from the embryo of the Enterprise Trust. At a later stage, a cultural and artistic stimulus was introduced and, eventually, social development was rekindled in order to allow the local people to gain maximum economic benefit from their collective effort.

The implementation of the Kiltimagh Business Plan saw a community-based company improve its financial assets from zilch to £300,000 in five years, leading to eventual ownership of workspace, houses and land. A review survey indicated that economic activity in the area increased, with 69 full-time jobs directly facilitated, and that banking activity increased by over 50 per cent. The town now has a new hotel, several new shops and a new streetscape. A new air of optimism has begun to establish itself in the town and district.

In endeavouring to change the economic order, Kiltimagh did not fall into the trap of being insular in its perspective. A farm-fresh food marketing company serving the broader region was established, as was a tourist-handling agency that promotes and sells products from the Shannon River to the Atlantic Ocean. A telematically controlled booking system with national and international potential was also devised.

Kiltimagh Economics became a national and international phenomenon and now over 1,500 community workers visit the area each year to witness the economic miracle. This gives credence to the principle of local autonomy, both administratively and financially.

The development of the arts in the area was no less a success story. The local community, reacting to the second phase of planning, undertook to change its image from a "back-woods" town to one associated with eminence in artistic pursuits. In its five-year programme, IRD Kiltimagh Limited decided that development of the arts and cultural activities was a key objective. This was undertaken as "An Dara Céim" (The Second Step) of the enterprise plan for the town and its environs.

The focus of "An Dara Céim" was two-fold, providing a basic infrastructure for the performing and visual arts, together with an emphasis on sculpture as a particular art form. The former railway station was converted into a unique sculpture park which comprises 12 beautiful pieces by well-known sculptors, set in a trail of artefacts and features, now restored to their former glory. Incorporated into the development is the town museum (formerly the goods store), a coffee shop and a workspace (formerly two railway carriages). This work had earlier been undertaken by the Kiltimagh Historical Society, and the official opening was performed by Boston businessman and ex-native, Tom Flatley, in 1989. New developments include the Artists' Exhibition Centre (formerly the stationmaster's house).

The adjacent Newtownbrowne School, which had previously been converted into a 300-seat Town Hall Theatre, was further developed to provide a self-contained artists' retreat, offering full self-catering facilities for visiting artists. Home-grown community arts programmes have been a feature of Kiltimagh life for a number of years.

In the past five years, Kiltimagh has "turned back the clock to go forward", by changing its townscape to the best of traditional. This work, under the guiding hand of Mayo County Council and a private architect, is continuing apace. In more recent times, Kiltimagh has adopted the theme "Kiltimagh — The Artisan Village".

Creating a brand-image for our towns and villages needs to be carefully considered by all communities. The need to nurture and preserve a distinctive local cultural identity cannot be over-emphasised. It was this principle that led me to push for such an identity to be created for Kiltimagh, and to seek to develop projects that were compatible with and complementary to the brand-image of the district.

The need for innovation in each community in order to fulfil its own individual needs is equally important. The process of merely replicating what the next community has been doing, without examining the prospect of adding value, will not provide a solid foundation for community enterprise. In the business world, the added-value principle is the hallmark of success. This principle, combined with the need to focus on a plan and avoid reactive management, is the best way forward. To be steadfast in this resolve requires a planned and integrated approach to community enterprise.

The employment of professional management, which perforce must be objective in its approach, requires that the manager must come from outside the community. The old adage that "no prophet is accepted in his own land" certainly applies to the difficult work of stimulating and guiding community enterprise. The case for Kiltimagh was made not only in the corridors of power in Dublin but directly in the decision-making process in Brussels. My impression was that I was perceived to be more objective in relation to the problems being addressed — and thus was always treated with more respect — than would probably have been the case had I been a native of Kiltimagh itself.

Above all, community enterprise is about local people contributing to the development of their own area in a planned manner. This book, in telling the story of Kiltimagh and what its community has achieved, gives an example of best practice in community enterprise — hence the title.

Section 1
Starting at the Atom

2
The Challenge to Change

"Kiltimagh of all places!" my mother exclaimed on that Saturday evening in November 1989 when I announced to her that I was abandoning my teaching post in Loughglynn to become General Manager of IRD Kiltimagh Limited. My mother had dropped in to my family-run food market in Ballyhaunis to pick up a few "goodies" for Sunday. I was the sole shop assistant for the late evening shift, having earlier that day completed a second interview with IRD Kiltimagh and signed a contract of employment. Little did my mother think, as she arrived on her weekly visit to see me in my 15-month-old business, that she would be told that another of her three sons was leaving the teaching profession, to which she herself had been so loyal. She had prepared her family to take up the reins of teaching, like my father and herself, and indeed my paternal grandfather and grandmother before. My leaving teaching, albeit temporarily, was difficult enough for her to absorb, but taking up a position "to develop the economic potential of Kiltimagh" was another matter. "And what will you do with Kiltimagh, Johneen?" was her first question, indicating some degree of acceptance of my new-found role. "Where will you get a factory or what?"

In these three sentences, my mother encapsulated all that needs to be said about the new task that I was about to undertake. She also encapsulated much of what people believe is the only essential requirement of economic development — the attraction of external investment.

It must be said that my mother was not being disparaging towards Kiltimagh or its people. Indeed she was born in Aughamore only a few miles from the town and would have regarded Kiltimagh almost as a home-town because of family ties and as a shopping centre. Instead, her remarks indicated the level of economic depression that had become associated with Kiltimagh. They also indicated the conversion to global economic thinking that had become commonplace and the equally dangerous presumption that "someone up there" would solve our economic problems for us.

Kiltimagh had been devastated by emigration and lack of internal investment. Derelict sites along the Main Street were commonplace. The town had lost its railway station in 1978 and its textile factory, employing 105, in 1983. My mother's remarks, then, were indications of an acceptance that towns like Kiltimagh were doomed to continue on a downward spiral towards economic extinction, and that the only salvation was the attraction of external investment.

Centralisation has created a sense of despair, isolation and apathy, as well as destroying ordinary people's faith in their ability to influence decisions that they believe could provide them with an opportunity to be part of the developing economy. It is a fact that the past 20 years have seen a gradual and steady increase in the influence of central government in Ireland. In all cases, power to implement schemes demands monetary resources. While decisions on the sharing of monetary resources must inevitably involve central government, there is absolutely no reason why the decisions on the types of schemes or policies appropriate to local areas should be centrally decided. It is an insult to local democracy and a reflection of local apathy that such impositions are accepted.

In my experience, the vast majority of state agency staff at regional and local level are competent people, genuinely concerned with improving the welfare of local communities and individuals. The experience of these people, their knowledge of the problems and their ability to find solutions are almost totally ignored, as scheme after scheme is devised at central government/state agency level and is handed down (in Moses-like fashion) on tablets of stone. Individuals, businesses and communities are sought to fit into schemes. Local empowerment would change this to allow suitable schemes to be sought for people, specific to their real needs. Indeed, the success of community initiatives and of small businesses in Ireland has very often resulted from state agency staff bending the rules and allowing common sense to prevail while risking being wrong-footed by their superiors.

On the other hand, increased centralisation has made the system less flexible and more bureaucratic, and it has increased the avoidance of real, definitive decision-making, through fear that mistakes might be made. Reduction of centralisation will beget reduction in bureaucracy, will beget greater local empowerment, will beget better use of state assistance, will beget less dependency, will beget greater economic diversity, and will eventually lead to spiralling development from the solid foundations of local economics.

The challenge to change the system is apparent. The need to change the system is apparent. The courage to change the system is not so readily apparent. Our politicians must take their courage in their hands. They must insist on real change and not perpetuate a charade of more reports, more boards, more musical chairs. This challenge to change is the greatest challenge facing community enterprise in Ireland today.

Redefining "Local"

The failure to solve the unemployment crisis in Ireland can be directly related to the failure of centralised economic planning. The number of people at work in Ireland declined, while other countries saw major increases in employment. The state has pursued a policy of support for large overseas multinational manufacturing while paying scant regard to the indigenous manufacturing or services sectors and, until recently, little or no regard to the real need to stimulate or help sustain smaller indigenous businesses. The service sector is ignored, with the exception of tourism. A business must "manufacture" to be entitled to any state assistance or to special reliefs in relation to Corporation Tax. This sectoral tampering has had detrimental effects, in that it encourages good service providers to lose focus and become manufacturers in order to share in the bonanza of state assistance to "industry". Efforts to redress this situation by way of County Enterprise Boards and Regional Development Authorities are only scratching at the surface of what must be done. The creation of further layers of co-ordination mechanisms, while refusing to recognise or consider the real requirements for local economic development, are indicative of a confused and nervous, if not actually a frightened, centralised government and political system. What is required is the empowerment of local communities and their involvement in integrated development planning. The concept of subsidiarity, whereby all administration occurs at whatever level it can be accommodated, must no longer be ignored.

The fact that no political party has seen fit to define "local" empowerment as anything more molecular than our local authority system is worthy of further examination. The real power still remains firmly vested in central government. The reins of power are held centrally. The crumbs — project-by-project development grants — are distributed to keep the "plebs" happy. Perhaps, in recent times, the crumbs have changed from bread to cake, but control of the bakery is never yielded!

The word "local" must now be redefined if real economic development is to occur. So also must the definition of "development" be challenged. Its true meaning is "having completed the job-in-hand". Its use in the context of the needs of local economies is misleading because it describes the end result. I prefer to use the words "local enterprise" to reflect the real task facing local economies.

The first requirement in local economies is constant stimulation of, and training for, innovative ways of using the indigenous resources, both physical and human. I have no doubt that with sufficient and well-planned innovation, real spiralling and self-sustaining development will occur at a pace that could never be matched by centralised planning, or by local authority schemes.

"Integration" is a third term worthy of definition when related directly to community enterprise. Experience shows that most local communities that have been successful have achieved a balance of emphasis between three very important aspects of local development, which are essential for a truly integrated programme:

(i)   Built Environment Renewal (BER)

(ii)   Local Economic Innovation (LEI)

(iii) Social and Cultural Stimulation (SCS).

To implement an integrated programme, new structures are required:

(i)   Professional management working with the voluntary sector

(ii)   Integrated action planning

(iii) Private funds as an acid-test of commitment by communities and the private sector, together with a global Innovation Fund from EU and state, using the broad statistics of public: 3, local community: 1, private business sector: 1.

To summarise, in the words of the Culliton Report:

> It is time for change. Time to realise that government on their own cannot provide us with secure jobs or a growing standard of living. Time to accept that the solutions to our problems lie in our own hands. We need to foster a spirit of self-reliance and a determination to take charge of our future. The next decade will provide greater opportunities for enterprise and initiative than we have ever seen.

To make it happen, the definition of "local" needs to be challenged and structures must be put in place and supported, which will allow a new flourishing of real "bottom-up" initiatives and will ensure that the community and its constituent parts are truly involved in decision-making and in the enterprise process.

3
Why Not Kiltimagh?

"Why Kiltimagh?" is a question often posed by those who have heard that "Kiltimagh is going well" and are inquisitive as to the reason. My usual retort is "because Kiltimagh people decided to make it happen, they put their money where their mouth is, and they planned to make change happen".

In coming to Kiltimagh as an outsider from "just over the road", I recognised its great community spirit. Kiltimagh also possessed another important ingredient to make community development a success: a very active pride-of-place. The third ingredient was an almost arrogant approach in demanding from on high what Kiltimagh needed — although, lacking focus and planning, and without a proven commitment to self-help, the arrogance had only led to annoyance in officialdom. By 1990, things were different. A prospectus was ready, prepared by the local community.

Kiltimagh Develops its Resources
The first phase of the Integrated Action Plan of IRD Kiltimagh Limited, "An Chéad Chéim" (The First Step) (1990–93), incorporated the following elements:

- Socio-economic programmes
- Community business projects
- Venture capital projects.

In "An Dara Céim" (The Second Step) (1992–95), the focus was on cultural/artistic development. "An Tríú Céim" (The Third Step) (1995–99) involved the team in planning a social programme to achieve greater participation by those termed socially disadvantaged. "An Cheathrú Céim" (The Fourth Step)

(1995–99) has addressed the overall framework development plan for "Kiltimagh — The Artisan Village".

As well as implementing these plans, working as a professional and voluntary team, IRD Kiltimagh endeavours to:

(i)   Generate, stimulate and support new ideas:

◊ Equity shareholdings were taken in small start-up companies.

◊ Security on loans and small grants was provided for others to get started.

(ii)   Provide employment via saleable services to the larger marketplace:

◊ Kiltimagh Data Services provides business bureau services within a radius of 20 miles.

◊ Greenfield Co-ordinators Limited provides technical advice and marketing assistance to small businesses and to communities throughout Ireland.

◊ Enterprise House and its annexe provides 4,000 square metres of workspace for small businesses, in units ranging in size from 50 to 600 square metres.

(iii)   Provide outward market linkages:

◊ This is an essential element to avoid job displacement. For example, Irish Farmhouse Variety Limited provides an opportunity for small food producers to market their produce under the brand-image "The Farmhouse Pantry"

◊ Naturally West Holidays provides a similar opportunity to the producers of tourism products by co-ordinating and selling packages (from the Shannon River to the Atlantic Ocean) to the non-English-speaking markets of Europe

(iv)   Provide opportunity for specific training needs:

◊ The John A. McNiece Training Centre, for example, worked with Coillte Teo and FÁS to train foresters; with Teagasc and FÁS to provide training for 26 fresh-food producers and a follow-on Product Development Officer to complete the packages; and with FÁS to provide business training skills for 25 traditional craft workers

(v)   Improve the physical infrastructure of the town and its environs:

◊ To make the ongoing economic development occur in a conducive environment

(vi) Increase awareness nationally, and in the EU, of the need to support local business and to shop locally, by organising a year-long local-spending campaign in Kiltimagh, and by organising the successful CUT campaign which has now been extended from County Mayo to other counties

(vii) Provide the infrastructure to foster the growth of cultural and artistic pursuits

(viii) Provide an opportunity for those termed "disadvantaged" to participate at all levels of activity.

Some figures may help to assess the effectiveness of this work:

	Targets set in Business Plan 1990–95	Progress against Targets 1994
Full-time jobs	30	69
Part-time jobs	67	52
FÁS Training Schemes	—	124

In July 1992, the UCD Environmental Institute was asked to assess the economic impact of this programme, based on jobs created to that date. It identified £600,000 of gross income generation (£463,000 net) and showed a gross output generation of £1.5 million with a multiplier of 1.15, giving a total spending effect of £1.8 million.

In February 1990, the two local banks provided evidence of their business activity. Four years later, the same banks showed an increase of 51 per cent in one case and 68 per cent in the other.

It is for this reason that *Section 2* of this book contains a case study of IRD Kiltimagh.

4

A Continuous Struggle to Survive

The first recorded reference to the town of Kiltimagh was in 1617. In 1685, it appeared as Cullineagh or Cullemagh. The Irish name of the town is Coillte Amach (Outer Woods). These woods were so called because they formed the western or outer extremity of the ancient forest. It is also thought by some that Kiltimagh comes from Coillte Mach, deriving in turn from Coillte Maghu. This is probable, since the old Irish name of the village of Kiltimagh is Coillte Magach, translated to mean "The Woods of Maghu".

Legend has it that Maghu was a Firbolg chieftain who fled the Battle of Moytura (circa 1,000 BC) and found a hiding place in the hills above the town. His grave is reputed to be the cairn grave located on the summit of the hill. This hill, in later years, earned the name of Sliabh Chairn.

Kiltimagh and Raftery the Poet

The Gaelic poet, Anthony Raftery, was born in 1784 at the foot of Lios Ard at the back of Killedan House. Nothing remains of the house, other than a stone slab, said to be the hearth stone, marked by a whitethorn bush.

Although blinded by small pox when he was nine years old, Raftery was said to be good at wrestling and other sports. He learned to play the fiddle and, according to local tradition, Mrs Taaffe of Killedan House was very kind to him. However, he was banished after an accident involving Frank Taaffe's favourite mare. He went first to Tuam but most of his life was spent between Loughrea and Gort, where he supported himself with his songs and music. He had no formal education but is said to have attended hedge schools whenever possible.

Over the years, he built up a formidable reputation as a poet, immortalising such beauties as Breegeen Vesey and Máire ní hEidhín. He was a man of the people and wrote about the Whiteboys, rack-rents and evictions. He died on Christmas Eve 1834, and is buried at Killeeneen, near Craughwell, County Galway.

Raftery is best remembered locally for his song praising the place of his birth:

> Cill Aodáin an baile a bhfásann gach nidh ann;
> Tá sméar 's subh chraobh ann 's measr' de gach sort.
> 'S dá mbéinn-se 'mo sheasamh 'gceart lár mo dhaoine
> D'imeodh an aois dom agus bhéinn ar's óg.

which translates to:

> Killedan (is) the village where everything grows;
> There are blackberries and raspberries and fruit of every kind;
> And if I were standing in the midst of my people
> Age would leave me and I would be young again.

Kiltimagh — The Artisan Village

Kiltimagh — The Artisan Village developed around the late nineteenth century, because of the efforts of Fr Denis O'Hara, who came to Kiltimagh as a young priest in 1875. Although only two years there, he began to bring Kiltimagh out of its poor and decayed post-Famine state.

A man of vision, enormous energy and buoyancy of spirits, Fr O'Hara started a lace-making industry and was responsible for the establishment of an agricultural bank, which gave grants for the building of walls to separate the people from their animals in the dwelling houses. He also organised the building of rows of houses (artisan dwellings) at Aiden Street and Thomas Street, which is Kiltimagh as we know it today. He built circular roads around the back of these houses to provide easier access for goods and materials.

Fr O'Hara collected money for his efforts by writing to many foreign and local newspapers, pleading for help for the poor of Kiltimagh. He also made contact with Kiltimagh's own emigrants in foreign parts. Thus the unpretentious hamlet of the

1870s was transformed into a busy active town.

By 1938, the village had a Catholic church, a police barracks, six public houses, three groceries, and a cloth shop. Thursday was Market Day, when corn, potatoes, pigs, butter and eggs were bought and sold. Houses were built by tenants for a lease of three lives, and were rent-free. The town had two schools at which the teachers were paid by the scholars. It had a small market square opposite the old parish church and parochial house at the south-western extremity of the town. Next to the square was a sand pit used for milling timber. Water supply was from the town well, situated 60 yards from the main street and reached by a steep narrow passage between the gables of the houses.

Fatal blows to the local economy came in 1978 — the closure of the railway station, on a section of track linking the Dublin–Westport and Dublin–Sligo line — and in 1983 when Irish Spinners — a textile factory — closed with a loss of 105 jobs.

As a result, Kiltimagh suffered economic stagnation and business decline. By 1990, in Main Street alone, over 40 per cent of the buildings lay derelict. Like all local economies, the prospects looked bleak.

However, the efforts of IRD Kiltimagh and the people of Kiltimagh changed all that in a few short years. The fruits of Fr O'Hara's labour are again evident in the Kiltimagh of today. The architectural outline, the market square and the shop façades reflect the style of its former glory as a market centre. The trades and crafts of the various artisans are being revived as a living experience. In conjunction with the visual restoration of the town, there is a complementary programme that endeavours to recall the ambience of the bustling market and artisan village and hinterland of previous centuries.

Location and Geographic Character

Kiltimagh is situated in a valley located in central-east Mayo between Sliabh Chairn to the west and Barnacougue to the east. Although not on any main route through the county, Kiltimagh is only 16 km from Knock International Airport and 8 km from the Marian shrine at Knock. The River Moy, known to salmon anglers all over the world, is just 10 km away.

In general, the land quality in the area is poor, so agricultural output is limited. Farm sizes are small and part-time farmers constitute a high proportion of those on the land.

Interestingly, while Kiltimagh is an archetypal inland town, which "turned its back on the river", it is considered by some to be an island territory. The island-territory theory is advocated by the best-known publican in the West of Ireland, my friend Gerry Walsh of the Raftery Rooms public house and diner. He correctly states that, to enter Kiltimagh, you must cross a bridge on every single approach road. In order to highlight this fact, he suggests that each bridge should have fuchsia planted beside it. I am certain that if Gerry were a younger man, given his particular pride in recent developments in the town, he would plant the fuchsia on the Kiltimagh bridges himself.

Kiltimagh and the "Culchie"

The term "Culchie" was recently added to the *Oxford English Dictionary* to describe "Irish country folk". The term originated in the 1950s from Kiltimagh and, up to recent times, was used as a derogatory term associated with the buffoonery of rough country fellows.

On the post-war building sites of Britain, the Kiltimagh native was a regular feature. The emigrants from the Kiltimagh hinterland who congregated together in the pubs with a large ethnic Irish clientèle became known as the "Culchies".

Later the term was used to describe all people of rural-Irish extraction. When adopted in Ireland, it was used by Dubliners to describe the many natives of rural Ireland. These "Culchies" flooded to the job in Dublin with the inevitable pull of central-ised administration systems.

Initially, "Culchie" was used as a put-down term. In more recent times, and in keeping with the fashion for environmen-tally friendly rural ways of life, the Culchie concept is being ameliorated and it has now become a source of pride to de-scribe oneself as a "Culchie".

In the 1970s Kiltimagh capitalised on the term and the "Culchie Come Home" Festival was a hugely successful event. In more recent times, Kiltimagh has developed its facilities in order to reflect the best of country life, with the objective of making the town of the "Culchie" the spiritual home of all country folk.

5
Soundings

The day after my mother was told of my new job, I stopped off for my customary Sunday post-golf apéritif in the local hotel and proudly announced to my colleagues my news of a change of career.

"So what will you be now?" asked the local vet.

"General Manager of a community company called IRD Kiltimagh," I retorted.

"But what will you generally manage?" came the inevitable question. And little wonder at the question, because we associate the term "management" with everything from large factories to large hotels to school management boards, but rarely, if at all, with management of the welfare of local communities.

The experiment to appoint a full-time manager to such a position as I had just accepted was unique in Mayo and rare enough in Ireland. The concept of full-time local community managers was being strongly advocated by the Irish Resource Development Trust of which Philip Mullally was the chief executive. In fact, assistance for community plans from this trust was conditional on:

- An integrated plan for economic development
- The appointment of full-time professional management.

This emphasis on supporting a process for development as distinct from a project-by-project support system was unique and was to have far-reaching effects for Kiltimagh. Unfortunately, the advantage of supporting such processes has still not received official public acknowledgement or sanction, except through the concept of Area Partnership Companies, which are still dominated by state-controlled mechanisms.

My First Decision

When I took up office in February 1990, Philip Mullally rec-
ommended that I immediately visit County Kerry and view the
work of our sister company IRD Waterville. This I did and
found that the company had become embroiled in a fish-
farming controversy in the locality, which was stemming its
effectiveness. I also found that management was left to do
much of the local everyday work, which I would normally have
associated with voluntary community endeavour. My other impression was one of management travelling throughout Ireland
spreading the IRD message to interested community development groups, thus limiting the work that could be done in Waterville.

This experience made me more determined than ever to:

- Take good soundings of the locals before committing the
  company to a plan of action
- Ensure that voluntary effort did not abdicate its role
- Stick to implementing the local plan.

Soundings

From the moment the IRD Kiltimagh office opened on the second floor of Kiltimagh Credit Union, the phone never stopped
ringing — I am glad to say that it hasn't stopped ringing since.

Many of the initial enquiries were of the type that bank
managers must surely experience on arrival to a new appointment: for example, whether we gave grants and loans. Some
off-the-wall ideas and a plethora of ideas that had been tried,
tested and had failed were also forthcoming.

We conducted a survey of the first 12 months of callers, and
found that in excess of 90 per cent were time-wasting from an
economic development point of view. Or were they? Personally,
I believe that they were useful in helping me to formulate my
own thoughts on what was needed, or what should be dis-
pensed with, in trying to create the economic development
stimulus demanded by my bosses. Every idea had some merit.
What was needed was to take the best ideas from "the think-
ers" and try and link them to "the doers".

Through local soundings, and with a minimum of theoretical
readings, and just one field trip, I slowly began to have a reali-

sation of what was needed for Kiltimagh. I began to ask myself and my board to define our vision for the area and where we saw Kiltimagh 10 years hence.

Being a pragmatist, I knew that Kiltimagh town, with its population base of 1,000, was never going to become the centre of the economic universe. Nevertheless, we decided to focus on a strong belief that "small is beautiful".

We ruminated over the strengths and weaknesses of small villages like Kiltimagh and determined that Kiltimagh had to find a niche in the marketplace by identifying certain gaps and focusing on these. It had to develop its facilities to become a pleasant place in which to live. It had to defend whatever facilities it had and not allow further essential services to disappear. It had to endeavour to prevent any further economic leakage by becoming a small, but complete, retail centre once again. Finally, it had to develop its own brand-image.

Developing a Theme

What gaps in the local economic order could be filled by an inland town like Kiltimagh? Why not start by providing a unique inland-tourism base with an emphasis on the traditional? Kiltimagh Historical Society had already provided a small museum on the theme of emigration. Mayo County Council, through its architectural office, suggested that the square be refurbished to reflect a traditional market square.

During my very first radio interview, which was on the occasion of the Philadelphia Quaker City String Band Concert (as part of the festivities for the Annual Festival of St Patrick), a representative from Ireland West Tourism referred to the rich cultural tradition of the area. He continued, "... and in fact this makes Kiltimagh an ideal candidate for the Bord Fáilte Theme Town Programme".

Ever desperate for a cue, I pursued the issue on the morrow and arranged an appointment with Ireland West Tourism. Two board members accompanied me to Galway. Much to our dismay, Ireland West Tourism had gone cold overnight on the idea. Dublin had spoken — Cong and Westport were to be the adopted Mayo towns for the Theme Town Programme.

"But Cong and Westport are beautiful — they have it made. Why not take on a real challenge like Kiltimagh? Why not give us some of the 75 per cent funding which is available?" we argued.

"We're sorry, we can't, but we know you're going to do it anyway," came the reply. A further meeting with the Bord Fáilte executive in charge of the Theme Town Programme confirmed the refusal.

On returning to base, and in the process of pursuing other aspects of development, I mentioned this episode to Sean Smyth of Mayo County Development Team. "Get the refusal in writing and possibly we can help," advised Sean. In truth, getting the refusal in writing proved almost harder than the opposite. Eventually it arrived.

Mayo County Development was as good as its word, and a grant was duly forthcoming to employ a private architect, John Halligan, to produce a plan to bring the Kiltimagh townscape back to its former nineteenth-century market-town appearance. As Michael Finlan of *The Irish Times* was to comment later: "Kiltimagh is winding back the clock to go forward."

This Theme Town plan was launched by Pádraig Flynn, then Minister for the Environment, in April 1992. In May 1992, by invitation, Mayo County Council held its monthly meeting in Kiltimagh. A motion to have the plan noted as a basis for planning and design was adopted unanimously.

Emphasising the Traditional

Gradually, and with pride, the face of Kiltimagh reflects a newfound emphasis. The beautiful bright appearance is a result of requests for colour-indexed paint schemes for buildings, offered as a service by the IRD office. The assistance of the LEADER programme in providing "sweeteners" for new shop fronts was also availed of.

After two years of constant negotiation and lobbying, Mayo County Council agreed to provide the funding to pay the ESB to place unsightly cables underground along Main Street. The agreement was that the community would provide a small amount of funding and that the new Town Enhancement Scheme, advocated by County Manager Des Mahon for all towns in the county, would be aggregated for a number of years in the case of Kiltimagh, to provide the sum of £70,000 plus.

Overhead traffic route lighting was also provided by Mayo County Council.

Traditional lamp standards for Main Street were provided by IRD Kiltimagh using a combination of LEADER grants and monies from the Irish American Partnership in Boston and the Friends of Kiltimagh in London. The support of the Irish American Partnership was enlisted, following a visit to Boston by the Chairman of IRD Kiltimagh, Brian Mooney, and myself, and introductions by Kiltimagh native, Tom Flatley. The Friends of Kiltimagh in London comprised many emigrants who organised events in the Irish Centre in Camden Town. Happily, some of these emigrants have since returned to live in their native place.

Completing the Transformation

In November 1993, through the good offices of Mayo Senior Tourism Officer Brian Quinn, Ireland West Tourism contacted me to indicate that there might be unspent, and potentially available, agri-tourism funds elsewhere in County Mayo. "I know you have plenty of plans," Brian said, "but do you have matching funds?"

A hastily convened meeting decided to approach our over-seas friends once again and to use a large portion of our own funds to finalise some much-needed ancillaries to our plan. New sections of the heritage trail needed attention and the artists' retreat park needed completion. A venture park as a unique attraction for youngsters was also planned.

A number of local farmers and rural-accommodation provid-ers agreed to lend support. Work commenced in November 1993 and was completed in two months. The sound of Sabbath-breaking JCBs was a regular feature throughout the area during those eight weeks.

Coming Full Circle

The reason I mention the above is that it was during the vari-ous discussions with Brian Quinn that we agreed to suggest a variation to Kiltimagh's nineteenth-century market-town theme. The theme we proposed, and which has since won local approval, was "Kiltimagh — The Artisan Village". And so it was that Kiltimagh came full circle to return to its former identity — a home for artisans and craftspeople as fostered originally by Fr Denis O'Hara in the late nineteenth century. So too had the wheel come full circle for Bord Fáilte, as it advocated, through Ireland West Tourism, a Theme Town image for Kiltimagh.

Firing on All Rockets

In the early development phase, a study of IRD Waterville was undertaken by the Irish Productivity Centre under the auspices of the Department of Finance. While we were never privy to its findings, we were asked to accommodate a visit from IPC representatives. Their advice can be summed up in two sentences: "Take the rifle approach to local economic development. The shotgun won't work." Needless to say, this advice was totally alien to my own views, though it was not too far removed from what a minority of my board of directors wanted to hear. I saw in the one project approach the danger of a one-project disaster, with inevitable consequences for Kiltimagh's last chance for survival.

Kiltimagh needed a major boost economically but not by firing a single rocket. A series of booster rockets fired together was the best chance. The physical infrastructure rocket, the slow firing of the strategic business rocket, the venture-capital rocket and a discreet injection of social/cultural rockets were all needed to fire the main spaceship of enterprise. Fortunately, the majority of our board of directors agreed with this format.

6
Leaking Resources

It is apparent that two types of leakage cause grave problems for towns like Kiltimagh.

In the case of Kiltimagh, the first problem was the Kiltimagh Diaspora. The 1988 survey of the same name, described in detail in *Section 2*, revealed a startling leakage of people. Though the haemorrhage of forced emigration had gradually tapered to semi-forced and semi-voluntary leakage, the "push" and "pull" forces of emigration had become embedded, leading to a habit of "doing what my brothers and sisters did".

Economic leakage was the second problem. Wage-earners in small businesses in the locality saw no anomaly in, on the one hand, their deep and sincere commitment to saving Kiltimagh and, on the other, driving to larger towns like Castlebar and Ballina and loading their cars with purchases that could be bought just as cheaply in shops and businesses in Kiltimagh.

It was estimated that over £2 million of a £6 million spend escaped annually from the local economy of Kiltimagh. Calculation of the jobs lost in the area because of the leakage made us realise that it was pointless continuing with an economic development campaign with an objective of creating more jobs locally, if we continued to shoot ourselves in the foot through economic leakage.

Do Your Shopping Locally

A massive change in attitudes was needed. A working group was formed among local traders. I sought the advice of a Ballaghdereen trader known to run good in-store promotions.

We decided to run the longest-running community shopping promotion in the history of the state. A twelve-month scheme was devised, based on assessments of local spending. Local businesses were asked to purchase tokens — 100 tokens for

£2.50 — which they then gave to customers — one token for every £5 worth of goods purchased. Monthly draws of tokens were held on the last Saturday of each month — outside the church after Mass, if weather permitted, or in some local hostelry. Prizes, which were generally sponsored, consisted of one prize worth in excess of £200 and four consolation prizes. The real attraction was that each of the five monthly winners became one of 60 eventual participants in a final draw for a new car.

Some businesses reacted with scepticism. Others were very supportive. The scheme was launched by Pádraig Flynn, then Minister for the Environment, who drew the first token on the occasion of the opening of the IRD Office in May 1990.

Rewarding the "Big Shopper"

One side-issue was the complaint of unfairness that only the five winners each month could be involved in the draw for the car. In order to meet the growing demand for greater opportunity of access for the car, we decided to introduce a "Big Shoppers' Incentive". We reduced the regular monthly draws to four general draws and one "Big Shoppers' Draw". The entrants to the Big Shoppers' Draw each month had to produce 100 ordinary tokens (proof of £500 worth of Kiltimagh shopping) in any one month. In return, their name was entered on a "Big Shoppers' Token". One token was drawn each month for a small consolation prize and an entry in the limited draw for the car. Everyone who swapped 100 general tokens for a Big Shoppers' Token also had the added advantage of having the 100 tokens included in the general monthly draw — effectively, a treble chance of winning in return for supporting local businesses.

The scheme was successful and certainly heightened awareness of the need to support local businesses. Radio and press interviews, which accompanied shopping-basket exercises of local versus large shopping-centre buying, also helped. The final draw for the car took place in June 1991.

Shop Local "By Degrees"

Christmas 1992 approached and I was engaged in casual pub-talk when a chance remark aroused my ire. It emerged that two coach-loads of shoppers had left Loughglynn (my former adopted town as a schoolteacher) on a spree to Galway. Immediately the mental arithmetic began — 100 shoppers spending £100 each meant that £10,000 was directly leaked from the small local economy of Loughglynn (a village of 100 inhabitants) on that one day.

While shopping sprees are exceptional, the repercussions for jobs for all small towns spurred me to contact Mid-West Radio and to issue a plea to shoppers to "wise-up and think local first" when shopping for Christmas. The reaction was immediate — one housewife later told me that she had heard my plea while en route to Galway and had done an about turn and returned to her local town to do her Christmas shopping — although not altogether positive from some surprising quarters. "Restricting the right to shoppers' mobility," said the President of Westport Chamber of Commerce on a radio interview, within hours of my initial statement.

Thinking on my feet, I advocated that shoppers should "think local by degrees" — referring to the need for shoppers to try to buy everything they could locally before shopping away from their home-base.

"But what about the housewife and value for money?" came the retort.

Ably supported by Tom Finn, President of Ballyhaunis Chamber of Commerce, I argued that value for money could also be got locally. We challenged local traders to react positively by giving value for money. We threw in the fact that people who went to larger centres spent more money than they intended, on impulse-buying and feeding the youngsters. "Ah, but sure it's a day out for the children," came the reply, and so on and on went the debate.

The Small Business Campaign

The Chairman of IRD Kiltimagh, Brian Mooney, indicated to me that this was the best thing we had ever done. We needed a working group. Within a week Brenda McNicholas, a housewife and mother of six, had taken charge. The first meeting of the Small Business Campaign took place on 16 February 1993 in Kiltimagh. In attendance at the meeting were shopkeepers and business interests from Swinford, Castlebar, Ballina, Clare-morris, Ballinrobe, Charlestown and Kiltimagh.

It was agreed to divide the campaign into three distinct parts:

(i) A public awareness campaign:

◊ To make the public aware of the effects of economic leakage from local economies and of the lack of a multiplier effect on income earned locally

(ii) A legislation campaign:

◊ To achieve the changes in law required to redress imbalances felt by small businesses, sole traders, small producers etc. in competition with monopolies

(iii) A retailers' awareness campaign:

◊ To build confidence that the Small Business campaign would succeed

◊ To improve existing services

◊ To focus the attention of suppliers on price anomalies.

The purposes of the campaign were outlined and agreed:

• Think local when you shop
• Spend your money in your local towns and with your local businesses
• Save local towns from dying
• Stop jobs being lost
• Save local services by supporting local businesses.

The consequences of inaction were listed:

• The demise of small towns in Ireland (already happening)
• Job losses
• Depopulation
• Emigration
• Closure of schools and workplaces
• Loss of facilities — for example, bank, post office, dentists, doctors.

On the suggestion of Francis McNicholas, the acronym CUT (Communities under Threat) was adopted as a name for the campaign. "CUT out the foolishness of economic leakage — realise your community is under threat" was the message.

It was also agreed that a role model would be developed for County Mayo and provided for other communities and counties to follow.

The CUT Campaign

The campaign was launched in Ballina on 1 April 1993. All Fools' Day was chosen to emphasise the foolishness of economic leakage from communities. The CUT campaign immediately grabbed the imagination on a national scale. Interviews on local radio and on the *Bibi Baskin Show*, the *Pat Kenny Show* and the *Gay Byrne Show* were all most professionally handled by Brenda McNicholas.

In an impassioned plea, Brenda wrote to shoppers:

Dear Shopper,

My name is Brenda McNicholas, housewife. My involvement in CUT arose from my voluntary work in my local town — Kiltimagh.

What have you noticed in your local town and region? Are shops closing? Businesses going bankrupt? Small producers "going to the wall"? Factories closing? Services disappearing? Ask yourself why this is happening.

CUT research has found the main reason: Money earned and generated locally is being vacuum-cleaned out of local economies into the foreign bank accounts of super-stores and monopoly operations.

Who is guilty? I was guilty.

Why? Because I was looking for better value on a fixed budget.

Let's discuss value. What is better value? For a moment, let's say we spend half our disposable income, say £75, shopping locally. The money stays in circulation, creates probably £110 in the process, boosts our local economy, helps create jobs, keeps our town viable and benefits us all. This is real value for money.

The same amount of money taken by the large

*multiples gives negligible economic benefit to your com-
munity. We never see the owner of these multiples, they
plough nothing back into our community. Is this real
value for money? Think about it.*

*We must stop and think. Money earned locally and
spent locally benefits us all. Nobody begrudges the odd
splurge elsewhere but please remember, when you're shopping, think local first and then as local as possible. Demand a better service and choice of goods (if necessary)
from your local retailers.*

*We all have experience of looking for sponsorship.
Where do we go? To our local shops and businesses, not to
the superstores. If we continue as we are, in ten years we
will have no small towns and businesses.*

*Let us not forget the poignant scenes at Knock Airport
at Christmas. Do you want to save your couple of pounds
now and lose your child to emigration a couple of years
down the road?*

*Think carefully before you shop. Do something positive
now. Get involved in CUT.*

Target groups for the campaign were also defined:

- General public: Civic-minded individuals concerned about
  the plight of small towns, and the consequences of inaction
- Teacher organisations: To increase awareness of the consequences of depopulation for rural schools, which is directly
  related to economic leakage. Teachers themselves should be
  concerned and be able to reflect this concern to their pupils
- Business people/employers/Chambers of Commerce: Who
  know the problem exists but feel helpless to redress the position
- Services sector: Who must realise the dependence of their
  sector on the survival of small businesses
- Employees of small firms: To make them realise that the
  consequence of their failure to support small businesses is
  the killing of their own jobs and the jobs of their children
- Legislators: Who must insist on the implementation of existing legislation and the need for further measures to protect
  small towns and communities

- Clergy: Whose influence can be significant and whose campaign via the Western Bishops' Initiative recognises these very difficulties

- Sports and cultural organisations: Whose ability to compete effectively and to survive depends on local sponsorship and local jobs

- Farmers/farming co-operatives: Whose concern on behalf of the farming communities must extend to the fight for the survival of small businesses, and family farms

- Unemployed: Job losses mean fewer prospects for those who are out of work and who are seeking re-employment.

While many journalists were impressed and supportive, none was more so than the critical and analytical Michael Finlan of *The Irish Times*. However, Michael Finlan wasn't supportive initially. In an early article, "Champions of Corner Shop Have Their Work CUT Out", he wrote:

> Unfortunately while CUT's objectives are worthy, I cannot see the movement achieving any great success. Even its own modest goal of persuading 15 per cent of shoppers to start buying regularly at the local shop may prove unattainable. The superstores are not villains, no matter what tactics they use to drum up business. They offer clean and attractive products and service in the most convenient way imaginable and, of course, what really makes them irresistible to people hard-stretched in making ends meet is that they really have found the way to keep their shelves stocked with goods that are consistently priced cheaper than anywhere else. This is what the small shopkeepers have to compete with, and they will have to offer something equally as good, or better, if they are to recover anything close to their former status. Let's hope they can. Perhaps they could start by uniting countrywide and forming a co-operative to go out into the marketplace to purchase their goods on as big a scale as superstores. That way they could at least equal their prices, if not under-sell them. And that's how you get the customers back.

The campaign eventually caught the attention of the Western bishops who were preparing a report, *Developing the West Together*. A statement of support was forthcoming from Dr Thomas Finnegan of Killala, who was particularly supportive of the idea of a "CUT Sunday" during which all churches would emphasise the CUT message.

Financial support for the campaign was secured from the large grocery wholesaling firm, Musgraves. The public awareness campaign was on a huge bandwagon of success.

Meanwhile, the retailers' awareness campaign floundered and had to be addressed while the legislation campaign conducted some initial forays. On 18 February 1993, Jim Higgins TD put the following question to Ruairí Quinn, Minister for Enterprise and Employment:

> *Question No. 12. Effects of Supermarkets.*
> Mr Jim Higgins asked the Minister for Enterprise and Employment if his attention had been drawn to the fact that the growing presence of large supermarket chains in rural Ireland is responsible for large-scale closure of small businesses and consequent loss of jobs; and if he will make a statement on the matter.

The Minister's reply boded ill for the efforts of CUT, as regards large supermarket chains, and showed a total indifference to the effects of economic leakage on rural towns and communities. He stated:

> I am not aware of any evidence to support the view that the growing presence of large supermarket chains in rural areas is responsible for large-scale closure of small businesses and consequent loss of jobs. A recent press article which I have seen in this regard would suggest that any businesses which have closed in such circumstances are those which are operating inefficiently or with high borrowings. The expansion of large supermarket chains into rural areas of Ireland, while it must be welcomed in the overall interests of the consumer, will inevitably give rise to increased competition for small business already established in those areas. Businesses which are inherently weak or inefficient will suffer most

from such competition. However, competition, as long as it remains within the law, must be welcomed. The Competition Act, 1991 prohibits anti-competitive practices and the abuse of a dominant position in the market. The Act applies to all sectors of the economy including the retail trade and leaves open to any person or business who is aggrieved by any anti-competitive activity prohibited under the Act to have direct recourse to the Courts.

Nevertheless, the local shopping campaign continued — it had to, if it were not to allow towns to die. The value-for-money issue had to be challenged within the ambit of the retailers' awareness campaign.

In the interim, advice was sought from various individuals on how to counteract the false impression that value for money could only be got in large business centres, and on how best to sell the message of CUT.

Mary Keane of Greenfield Co-Ordinators, Kiltimagh (a community and business development consultancy that grew from the activities of IRD Kiltimagh) advised that two messages should be constantly emphasised:

(i)   What is Better Value? Do you want to save your pound now and lose your child to emigration a couple of years down the road? Meanwhile, the poignant scenes at Knock Airport each Christmas should be emphasised.

(ii) Emphasise the fall-out of centralised shopping on the rural villages of continental Europe. Quoting Michael Finlan again:

> Mass exoduses on the weekend or on seasonal shopping sprees could eventually reduce small towns and villages to a moribund state, he (Higgins) predicted. Who's to say he's wrong? It has already happened on the Continent: a striking thing about the many villages in the South of France is that you will hardly ever see anybody on the streets, no matter what time of day.

Since the inception of the CUT concept, Brenda McNicholas has travelled throughout Ireland, addressing community and business groups and national conferences such as the ICA and teachers' conferences. Her purpose is to bring the CUT message to those who can influence others regarding the need for such a campaign and the consequences of inaction. The failure of many retailers to recognise the potential of such a campaign is disappointing. What is required is a huge change of attitude and a change in our culture to instil loyalty and solidarity. There is a need for the CUT message to be constantly hammered home until it sinks in.

Community leaders in Ireland would do well to study the success of the Mondragon Co-operative in the Basque region of Spain. There, the culture of solidarity with the development of the region has seen a small community co-operative flourish to a membership of 25,000 people employed in a multimillion-pound business, engaged in financial services, manufacturing and retail distribution throughout Spain and farther afield.

Official acknowledgement of the principle of the CUT campaign must also be sought by way of stated government policy and schemes. This should take the form of a reorganisation of our small towns, which were planned to cater for an earlier era, to change them for a very different economic order. An incentive scheme to achieve this should be proposed in a creative manner by our Government to the European Commission. The scheme would restimulate local towns and prepare them to meet the needs of the communities they seek to serve in the year 2000 and thereafter. Such changes can only be achieved in a decentralised regional development programme.

Time is running out for the small towns of rural Ireland. For everyone's sake, all who care about the preservation of our rural way of life should support CUT now.

7
Fission and Bloody Committees

My first interview for the position with IRD Kiltimagh came about after I replied to an advertisement placed by Western Management Consultants, Galway. The interview panel comprised four people with an array of local, independent and professional expertise — indicative of the professional manner that IRD Kiltimagh intended to adopt in approaching the challenge of local enterprise.

Immediately on completion of my second interview for the position, which took place in the local curate's house and which included a computerised personality profile test, I was informed that I had got the job, and I was invited to sign a contract of employment two hours later.

I then met the Local Committee of the Board of Directors. To my recollection, all eleven members chosen to represent the community, until the first AGM of the company 15 months later, were present at this introductory session.

My introduction to the full board of directors, including state agency representatives, took place later in January 1990 and prior to my taking up duty. This was to fulfil the legal requirements of board approval.

I met regularly with the Local Committee. Though the eleven members were enthusiastic for the success of the IRD initiative, gradually I began to realise that this Local Committee, with one or two exceptions, did not visualise itself as a project implementor. Neither was there any serious commitment to involving the broader community in project development. Instead, the Local Committee saw itself as my management team, which would dictate the pace and the type of project to be undertaken. They were terribly conscious of the "knockers" and absolutely fearful of failure, knowing that they were the "scapegoats". In all of this, the Chairman, Brian Mooney, and a handful of others were towers of strength.

The opposite situation prevailed at board meetings. With the involvement of state agency representatives, broader views were taken. New projects and the pace of projects caused no problems, except for some small degree of consternation at the quantity of proposals.

The Enterprise Centre Debate

At our first meeting, the board informed me that preliminary research had been undertaken into the provision of an enterprise centre, and some cost details were provided in writing for my perusal. It was decided that a feasibility study should be undertaken to examine the options.

The results of my study generated serious debate. I advocated the purchase of three semi-derelict buildings in the town and their refurbishment into 1,000 square metres of workspace. The Board of Directors agreed to support the proposal. The IDA Regional Office in Galway approved a grant of £97,000. Deposits were paid. But the project continued to give rise to heated debate at Local Committee meetings.

Many local issues, which so often surface and destroy community initiatives, emerged during this stormy debate on the enterprise centre project. The reasons advocated for not proceeding ranged from the fact that the buildings to be purchased had been on the market for years, to the unsuitability of the site, to the possibility of having the centre on a greenfield site, to the need to build a costly retaining wall on the site — even to the advisability of having a centre at all.

Eventually, some Local Committee members indicated to the IDA that they were unhappy with my study. This not only put a question mark over the integrity of my work, but also reflected on the work of the IDA itself, which had approved both the study and subsequent funding. The local banks heard of the controversy and ran for cover. Refusals to "fund community projects which are the subject of interest-bearing debt" arrived in writing.

An extraordinary meeting of the board was called to discuss

the objections. Many of the state agency representatives absented themselves from what would obviously be a tense meeting. One who did attend and voiced his opinion unequivocally was Vincent Roche, Manager, North-Western Fisheries Board. Eventually, a compromise was proposed. The accounting firm, Stokes Kennedy Crowley, was to be asked to act as an independent arbitrator in the dispute. After the meeting, I called to the offices of Stokes Kennedy Crowley in Galway. A minimum fee of £3,000 was mentioned. The first AGM of the company came in the intervening period and agreed to change the management structures. A revitalised board, at its next meeting after the AGM, rescinded the decision to seek an independent arbitrator and agreed to proceed with the project forthwith.

The Company Chairman Brian Mooney, and Company Secretary Padraic Brennan, agreed to approach some business people in town to see whether they would act with them as guarantors for £100,000. Half of this amount was required for guarantee on a bridging loan, the other half on a more permanent basis. Three further guarantors were found in the persons of Joe Mulhern, Francis McNicholas and Patrick McNicholas.

Winning £60,000 in the ESB Community Enterprise Awards in September 1991 allowed the Board of Directors to repay the mortgage, release the guarantors from all obligations, and secure the deeds for the company. The project was saved and Enterprise House was officially opened by President Robinson on 28 July 1994.

Involving the Community

I was very conscious throughout my first year in office that the broader community of Kiltimagh was not participating in the activities of the company. The attitude was to "leave it to the IRD". The attitude of a large section of the IRD management was to "leave it to the manager", who was being paid to do the work. It was obvious that, in attempting to create a bottom-up approach to development, and through the selection of a board of directors and a manager, a new top-down approach had been unconsciously created.

To change this, we suggested a working group system, with:

(i)   Three members per group

(ii)   A leader, to undertake projects, who would:

◊ Attend working group meetings

◊ Report on their project to the joint-chairmanship of the IRD Chairman, representing the voluntary sector, and the manager, representing the professional sector.

Following the establishment of the working group system, anyone who asked "Why isn't IRD doing that?" was instructed to establish a working group and told that IRD management would facilitate their development proposals, if these were feasible.

Each working group clearly understood that its project had to be self-sustaining. Grants could be sourced with the help of the IRD office, but no monies would be paid out of central funds except to trigger projects. Such "trigger" monies had to be returned to central funds. This approach differentiated the genuine project leaders from the off-the-wall suggestions.

At one stage, no fewer than 26 working-group leaders were attending meetings and reporting on their projects. Most of these leaders were not members of the board of IRD Kiltimagh. This to me was the ultimate proof that the IRD system could be truly community-driven and could become a real bottom-up development. In fact, the real acid-test of community involvement lay in the fact that membership of the board of IRD Kiltimagh was less obvious than involvement in IRD Kiltimagh working groups.

The Benefits of Meetings

Meetings of the working groups had other beneficial effects:

(i)   They provided a community communications channel on IRD projects whereby each leader heard the progress of all other projects.

(ii)   They provided an impetus to have progress to report on each project, since progress was recorded and a general memo of meetings was sent to all. Hence, failure to make progress between meetings was evident.

(iii) They provided an opportunity for professional management and voluntary workers to meet and debate project development and progress.

(iv)   They provided management with a knowledge of the difficulties being experienced in project development and an opportunity to alleviate some of these.

(v)   They provided an opportunity for a sense of fellowship to develop between project leaders and also with management.

(vi)   They had a limited time span, as projects were specifically related to short time-frames. Every leader knew that they would not have to look after the project indefinitely. Projects were geared towards finishing dates and attendance at working group meetings ended when the project was complete.

As an aside, the written assessment of a Maynooth College Diploma group, who visited Kiltimagh for a number of days as part of their community development studies, made interesting reading. The assessment asked, "What did you find most beneficial from your visit?" The answers from three different assessment sheets stated: "The women's working groups in Kiltimagh".

I found this interesting from two points of view:

(i)   A realisation of the predominance of women in undertaking and completing projects in Kiltimagh

(ii)   The new found involvement of women in the workings of IRD Kiltimagh.

No More Committees!

If you ask Brian Mooney why we insisted on using the name working groups, you will get the crisp retort: "No more committees. Committees mean power. We've seen enough of bloody committees!"

8
What is There to Tell?

One of the obvious conflicts that can arise between professional community management and voluntary community working groups relates to the amount of information that needs to be released:

- To the broader community being served
- To the general public.

Personally, I dreaded having to face this dilemma, as I genuinely believe that if the story is good enough, it will tell itself because it will be sought after. But in order to justify its existence to a small local subscriber base, information must be supplied by the enterprise mechanism.

There are many ways in which this can be done. Bush-telegraph via local gossip and pub-talk seemed the most attractive to me. This avoided the danger of putting something in writing that might not happen. It also allowed for "kite-flying" and "testing the wind" on new ideas and provided an opportunity to assess the reactions to decisions, either recently made or about to be made. We were fortunate too, in our early days, to have ready-made access to the parish newsletter.

The general public was also curious. Within one month, I had completed interviews with RTE's Western correspondent, Jim Fahy, the *Western People* newspaper and two interviews on Mid-West Radio. This thirst for news on the part of the general public frightened me a little.

Accordingly, I made a specific request to my board to allow me to keep IRD Kiltimagh out of the public eye, until we had formulated definite plans, and until we were sure what plans we could bring to successful conclusions. The effects of this were two-fold. Keeping out of the public-eye relieved the pressure for answers, while the bush-telegraph worked wonders locally. Meanwhile, the real work of planning continued apace.

One downside of keeping all your announcements until success is in sight is the danger of depleting the subscriber base because of adverse local comment on an apparent lack of progress. Another downside of being media-shy is that when plans are formulated and ready for formal announcement, the number of good ideas they contain can lead to a loss of impact.

Nevertheless, I believe that, as a general principle, announcements on community development plans should only be issued when sufficiently weighted with innovation or with economic or social comment. In general, the rule is that if the story is good enough, it will always tell itself. Better to be sought after for news, than to seek every opportunity to feign newsworthiness.

Share the Glory

Another policy that I was determined to pursue was to allow as much kudos as possible to fall to the local community. The fact that community achievements are just that, and that professional management is paid to bring these about, means that the voluntary community worker deserves to get the praise, the photographs in the newspaper, and the press or radio interview. Unless there is a more global content to be emphasised or criticised by way of broader policy decisions, or perceived threats to the operational structures within which professional management must operate, this policy is a good one for professional managers to bear in mind.

There were occasions where this did not always operate, sometimes because local radio interviewers in particular would target professional management as being the most accessible. In general, however, a reticence to be up front and in the limelight is a better policy for professional management. I purposely dodged press conferences or launches when the working group was able to perform adequately in my absence. I usually did this by taking a strategically-timed break.

Charge for Information

To ensure that the first two years of planning and implementation were not wasted on invitations to speak all over the country, we decided that any group or person who wanted to hear what we were doing could come to Kiltimagh to hear the story — instead of us going to them. The board supported this policy and agreed to impose a charge on external presentations. The number who came to see our development programme is significant. At least 1,500 people came to Kiltimagh in both 1993 and 1994, solely for this purpose.

We only imposed a nominal charge on such groups, as we felt that it was publicity for Kiltimagh. We hoped that as visitors, they would spend some money on food, fuel or some such. Many who came were either students of community development or community development groups. In more recent times, a policy of charging visiting groups who were already paying a hefty fee to a consultant developed, as the plagiarism of ideas by consultants became apparent.

Our foreign visitors have come from as far afield as Guadeloupe, Greece, France, Slovenia, Wales, England, the USA and Pakistan.

On the home front, our visitors have included Maynooth College students, FÁS regional managers, County Agricultural Officers, and development groups from Roscommon Town, Feakle, County Clare; Kinlough, County Leitrim; Ballymore, County Longford; Inishowen, County Donegal; Draperstown, County Tyrone; Strokestown, County Roscommon; Duhallow, County Cork; Lough Arrow, County Sligo; and Keenagh, County Longford.

Presentations have been provided in places as far away as Garretstown, County Cork; Rathdrum, County Wicklow; Ballinasloe, County Galway; Roscommon Town; and Strokestown, County Roscommon.

Media Coverage

And the story told itself. Most newspapers have covered aspects of our development programme. A short selection of some comments is worth reproducing to illustrate their views.

In 1993, a new publication, *Weekender West*, stated:

> Historically, Kiltimagh has two great claims to fame. It was the birthplace of the blind poet, Anthony Raftery, sometimes referred to as the last great bard of the

people, and it also has the somewhat dubious distinction of being the origin of the word "Culchie". Nowadays, however, it is fast becoming a vibrant and forward-looking town being the location for one of the country's more successful examples of integrated rural development.

The *Western People* (1993):

> "The projects I have seen on the ground here are very good, practical examples of what can be achieved by the right kind of motivation, programming and funding," said the Minister of State at the Department of Agriculture, Mr Liam Hyland.

The *Western People* (1993):

> "Instead of being a no-hope town, Kiltimagh is now regarded nationally as the living proof that our rural towns can survive, that rural communities can prove that self-help is the only way to get the job done," commented an impressed Fr Harry Bohan at the Annual General Meeting of IRD Kiltimagh Limited.
>
> "It is a miraculous performance. I used to come in one end of this town seven or eight years ago and couldn't get out the other end fast enough. I must now add a word of caution. Kiltimagh was never at a cross-roads before, but it is at a cross-roads now. Yes, Kiltimagh can now prove the lie to the cynics who say that it will all fall apart after a few years of excitement, it can now go from strength to strength proving that your town has a community spirit that is rare.
>
> "Alternatively you can help this effort to become paralysed. Do you want the Kiltimagh of 1988 or the Kiltimagh of 1993 with its plans to the end of the century? The choice is yours — but you also have a moral duty to choose wisely," concluded Fr Bohan.

Headline in the *Connacht Telegraph* (1991):

> Positive, Professional Kiltimagh Plan Gets Results.

The *Western People* (1991), from Brendan Forde in an article headed: "Suas go dtí £50,000 ag dul go Coillte Mach":

> If most towns in Ireland discovered that nine out of ten
> school-leavers were emigrating, there would be much
> anxiety and concern about the future. Of course, if this
> fact were added to a tradition of heavy emigration from
> an area, then people might really become worried and
> even despair. To finish a town, if the news that the major
> employer in the area were asking questions about its fu-
> ture commitments to jobs, then many a person might just
> decide to close up house and emigrate to somewhere with
> a little more hope. All of these misfortunes have, indeed,
> happened in Kiltimagh, and a survey in 1989 came up
> with depressing findings. An IRD company was formed
> and an efficient man was appointed to head it and before
> long a plan was in place to reverse the East Mayo town's
> fortunes. The ESB Award could mean £50,000 for Kilti-
> magh, and it was a proud day for the town, as the Presi-
> dent lauded their efforts at revitalising the local economy.

The Irish Times (1991), from Michael Finlan:

> A series of articles in *The Irish Times* in 1989 graphically
> detailing the social damage inflicted on Kiltimagh by un-
> employment and emigration roused the Mayo town into a
> spurt of activity which last night won it a major award
> for enterprise. Kiltimagh is winding the clock back to
> move forward. Kiltimagh has started to move with the
> times.

The *Sunday Business Post* (1992), from Kathleen Barrington:

> The people of Kiltimagh are the first to admit that in
> 1988 their town seemed to be in terminal decline. There
> were more deaths than births, houses stood derelict and
> the town's two hotels were both for sale. Now Kiltimagh
> is considered a role model for other communities seeking
> to develop their area.

Letter to the *Western People* from Cormac O'Hora in France
regarding the debate on the definition of the word "Culchie",
which had earlier been reported as being inserted into a draft

of the *Oxford English Dictionary* as "a rough country fellow":

> Local businessman, John Higgins, says: 'Townspeople feel it an unfair and unflattering definition and we have sought to have it changed'. Their complaints have been endorsed by Pádraig Flynn, the Irish Environment Minister, and the editors are now reviewing their initial definition. "We will take on board the observations of the people of Kiltimagh," says a spokeswoman.
>
> I have no doubt that your readers, especially in Kiltimagh, will be interested to know that this controversy has now attracted the attention of one of the world's best-known newspapers, the *Times* or so-called "Thunderer". I don't suppose that any other town in Mayo is the object of so much attention in high places. Undoubtedly, one happy outcome to this publicity would be investment and job creation in the area. Hopefully, that will come.

The *Irish Farmers Journal* (1992), from Sonia Kelly:

> "Culchie" used to be the term to denote someone from the backwoods and was derived from the name Kiltimagh, a country town in Mayo. Today, these so-called Culchies have turned the tables on those urban smart-alecs who coined the phrase, by producing and marketing what everybody is clamouring for nationwide and that is real food, as opposed to the mass-produced product. Real "green" home-grown, nourishing and flavoursome stuff, without the addition of any sinister "E"s.
>
> Now Kiltimagh, it must be admitted, is in a disadvantaged area with minimal prospects in industry. Left to outside patronage, the outlook was pretty bleak, so they asked themselves what was available already that was marketable. They soon realised that the answer was staring them in the face: they had uncontaminated land and a great many of them were skilled in husbandry. If they co-ordinated production, did they not have a valuable commodity? When one thinks about it, does not all of the West of Ireland have this same potential for fresh-food enterprises?

Section 2
Integrated Resource Development: A Case History

9

The Spark that Lit the Fire

IRD Kiltimagh Limited has as its primary objective "the development of the economic potential of Kiltimagh and its environs to the fullest, and in a way that will benefit the whole community". All of its more immediate objectives serve this one.

The company was launched in response to a cry of desperation from a community devastated by the plague of emigration, the effects of which were confirmed by a detailed survey initiated by local curate, Fr Padraic Brennan. Focusing on what happened to young people after they completed their second-level education, the survey showed an alarmingly high level of emigration from the area — 38 per cent in the age group 19–28. Another aspect of the survey showed that, over a nine-year period, 63 per cent of school-leavers had been forced to leave the area. Three-quarters of these had been forced to leave Ireland. It was also estimated that the figures only represented half of the total emigration of all age groups from the area.

Background to the Survey

In 1988, the pupils of St Louis Secondary School, Kiltimagh, together with local curate, Fr Padraic Brennan, undertook a youth migration survey entitled "The Kiltimagh Diaspora".

It was widely recognised that Kiltimagh and similar-sized towns in the West of Ireland had gone through a period of economic stagnation and business decline. Official statistics revealed that Kiltimagh had a population of 982 in 1986, which represented a drop of 14.2 per cent on the 1981 figure. Between 1986 and 1991 the decline had slowed, with the 1991 Census revealing a population of 952 (a drop of 3 per cent).

Kiltimagh town is situated in what had become known locally as "The Black Triangle" of Mayo, encompassing the area within a triangle formed by the towns of Kiltimagh, Charlestown and Swinford. The land quality is poor and agricultural output is limited as a result. Farm sizes are small — the average farm size is less than 14 hectares — and part-time farmers constitute a high proportion of those on the land. A large percentage of the population is dependent on social welfare assistance. There is an absence of any obvious natural resources normally associated with enterprising potential. The town is situated inland — too far from the sand and sea — and has no large mountains in the immediate vicinity.

While many towns, most notably the "Bally" towns of Ireland, are situated on rivers, Kiltimagh town had turned its back on the small rivers of the Pollagh and Glore. Kiltimagh has no large estates to remind it of the landed gentry, since land had been sub-divided to meet the needs of the small farmers of the area. Kiltimagh is the only inland Mayo town with a population of circa 1,000 that has neither a national primary nor a national secondary route passing through it to provide the economic boost normally associated with these throughways.

For the increasingly mobile shopper, the pull to the larger urban centres of Castlebar and Ballina had hastened the demise of villages such as Kiltimagh as early as the mid-1970s. The resultant lack of incentive to re-invest in businesses was also a contributor to the downward economic spiral.

Nobody Shouted "Stop!"

In the 1970s, when the late John Healy penned *Nobody Shouted 'Stop!'* about his native Charlestown, he was regarded as a prophet of doom. Today the truth of Healy's foresight is obvious throughout rural Ireland. Gradually, the small towns and villages of the West of Ireland have become "tombstone villages".

Kiltimagh was facing a certain future of derelict sites, empty houses and closed business premises. Its population was facing the increasing costly, although not altogether unattractive, prospect of travelling to nearby large commercial centres for most of its needs. It was in this context that the youth migration survey — Kiltimagh Diaspora — was undertaken.

The Kiltimagh Diaspora Survey

"Diaspora" means dispersion, though it has a special significance with regard to the dispersion of the Jews in Biblical times. It is used here to sum up what has happened in recent years to the youth of Kiltimagh and surrounding districts.

The purpose of the survey was to identify the trends in employment, unemployment, location and education among youth up to the age of 25 or 26. Subjects for the survey were the past pupils of two second-level schools in Kiltimagh — St Louis Convent Secondary School and Coláiste Rafteirí Vocational School. Apart from Kiltimagh and district, the schools' main catchment area extends to Knock, Kilkelly and Bohola, as well as the fringe areas of Swinford, Balla, Aughamore and Ballyfarna. The number known to have begun second-level education and left it since 1973 came to 722. The results of the fieldwork survey in ascertaining information were encouraging with a 91 per cent response.

Kiltimagh Diaspora — Summary of Findings

Educational Patterns

The survey revealed some interesting statistics for the period. At 79 per cent, the figure for those sitting the Leaving Certificate was 12 per cent higher than the national average. This trend was in keeping with other parts of the West of Ireland, where 77 per cent overall went on for Leaving Certificate qualifications. Some 71 per cent of the parents of these pupils had primary education only; as few as 17 per cent of parents had attempted the Leaving Certificate themselves and just 5 per cent had any kind of third-level education.

Occupation of Parents

The survey showed the expected traditional pattern of farmers (51 per cent of fathers) and farm-help/housewives (83 per cent of mothers). Surprisingly, only 1 per cent of fathers were unemployed.

One Year After Leaving Second-Level Education

The survey showed that in the year immediately after leaving school, almost half the boys (44.5 per cent) and almost three-quarters of the girls (72 per cent) were engaged in further education. Almost half the boys (45 per cent) had jobs, while just under a quarter of the girls (24 per cent) were employed.

Occupation of Parents	Fathers %	Mothers %
Farmers	51.0	2.5
Business	17.5	3.5
Construction	10.0	3.0
Services & Other	5.5	1.0
Bakery & Other	4.5	1.0
Professional	3.0	4.0
Factory	2.0	10.0
Unemployed	1.0	Nil
Farm-Help/Housewife	Nil	83.0
Deceased	5.0	2.0
Total	**99.5**	**110.0**

Note: Some mothers chose two categories to describe their occupations indicating part-time working.

Situation One Year After Leaving School	Boys %	Girls %	Total %
Further Education	44.5	72.0	59.0
Employed	45.0	24.0	34.0
Unemployed	10.5	4.0	7.0

Employment

There was a significant reduction in the number of girls seeking clerical employment — down from approximately 50 per cent in the 1978 Leaving Certificate to approximately 10 per cent in 1984.

Marital Status

One in five (19 per cent) of those surveyed were married.

Migration / Emigration

Covering school-leavers over a 14-year period, the survey showed that 37 per cent remained in their home area, 63 per cent had gone away (7 per cent to Dublin, 18 per cent elsewhere in Ireland, 38 per cent emigrated).

Between June 1986 and November 1987, emigration among the group surveyed increased by 9 per cent. Almost three-quarters (71 per cent) of all emigration has been to the UK, 25 per cent to the USA, and the balance elsewhere.

Research indicated that it is probable that in the preceding year, in the 18–27 age group, 1,500 left Mayo, 5,500 left Connaught, and 48,000 left Ireland. In all age groups, it is probable that 2,225 left Mayo, 8,250 left Connaught, and 72,000 left Ireland. This gives an annual rate of emigration more than twice the officially accepted figures.

The community, both in Kiltimagh and more widely, reacted with shock and alarm to the results. The survey and its effects were the feature of a series of articles in *The Irish Times*. It was clear that something had to be done — before it was too late!

10

A Model for Development

In 1988, the Mayo County Development Team published a report (*The Moy Catchment's Future*), prepared by Philip Mullally BE, Chief Executive of the IRD Trust. The IRD Trust is based in Dublin, and has as its overall aim "to create sustainable employment in specific areas in Ireland, through a 'bottom-up' integrated approach, involving local people and state agencies working together and achieving a consensus on development and resource enhancement".

Inspired by this report, a local group of community activists considered the establishment for development of a "third-sector" company, thus adopting an OECD model of development that was one of the recommendations of the Mullally Report.

Company Prospectus (1989)

A Company Prospectus for IRD Kiltimagh Limited was launched in July 1989. I was appointed as a full-time manager in February 1990, working from an office sponsored by Kiltimagh Credit Union. The company later acquired its own office in the refurbished Enterprise House. This office now has a complement of six full-time positions as follows:

- General Manager
- Administration/Rural Resettlement Officer
- Business Enterprise Officer/LEADER Project Manager
- Tourism Enterprise Officer
- Social Enterprise Officer
- Office Secretary.

Action Plan (1990)

A visionary document was launched in July 1990 under four categories of enterprises:

(i)   Alternative Farm Enterprises

(ii)   Tourism

(iii) Small Businesses

(iv)   Infrastructural Projects.

An Chéad Chéim (1991)

The first step in the Strategic Plan was launched in February 1991. It contained three main enterprise categories:

(i)   Community Enterprise Programme

(ii)   Company Business Projects

(iii) Venture Capital Projects.

The Development Process

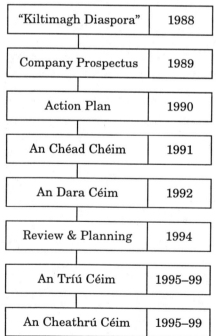

"Kiltimagh Diaspora"	1988
Company Prospectus	1989
Action Plan	1990
An Chéad Chéim	1991
An Dara Céim	1992
Review & Planning	1994
An Tríú Céim	1995–99
An Cheathrú Céim	1995–99

An Dara Céim (1992)

The second step in the Strategic Plan towards a Cultural/ Artistic Stimulation programme was launched in July 1992, containing four parts:

(i)   The Kiltimagh Community Arts Programme

(ii)   The Kiltimagh International Sculpture Symposium

(iii)   The Kiltimagh Theatre & Artists' Retreat

(iv)   The Kiltimagh Artistic and Cultural Centre.

Funding

The general administration of IRD Kiltimagh Limited was funded mainly by the local community in the parish of Kiltimagh (approximately 2,500 in population). By direct subscription, the community subscribed over £111,000 over a four-year period to fund the company.

The IRD Trust, which is now incorporated into the Enterprise Trust, subscribed £90,000 to fund the integrated development plan of the company. Mayo County Development Team, the Industrial Development Authority and FÁS assisted with general administration funding of management and staffing.

The company is incorporated and limited by guarantee, thereby being non-profit-making and having subscribers as distinct from a share capital base of equity.

Categories of Directors

The Board of IRD Kiltimagh Limited comprises three categories of Directors:

- Eleven elected by the local community at the AGM

- Three co-opted from the private sector of business and commerce

- Six invited representatives of state agencies and Local Authorities.

Administrative Channels

The following administrative channels have evolved over the past four years:

- Voluntary/Professional Sector Administration Structure
- Professional Facilitation Structure
- Communications Systems
- Network of Support Agencies — Funding and Expertise.

Voluntary and Professional Sector Administration Structure

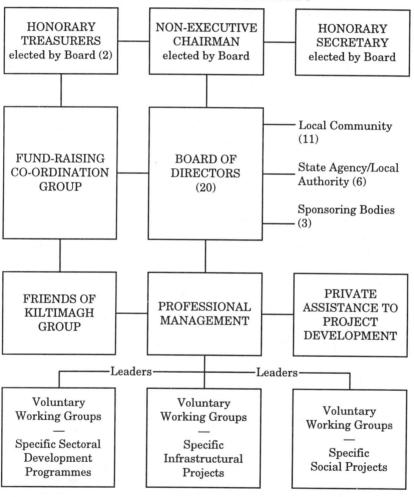

Professional Facilitation Structure

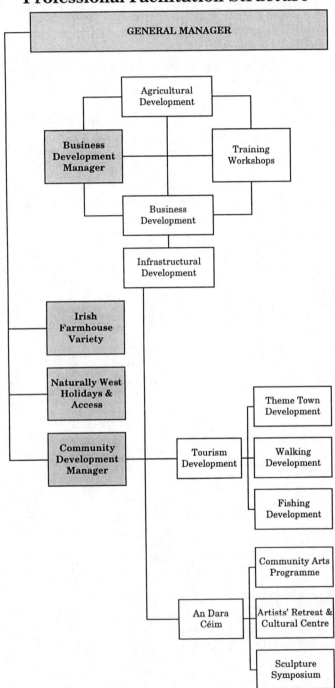

Management Communication Systems

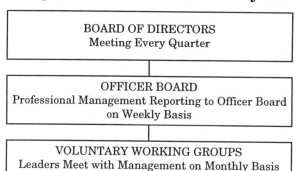

BOARD OF DIRECTORS
Meeting Every Quarter

OFFICER BOARD
Professional Management Reporting to Officer Board
on Weekly Basis

VOLUNTARY WORKING GROUPS
Leaders Meet with Management on Monthly Basis
Specific Meetings, as Appropriate

Network of Support Agencies
Funding & Expertise During Period

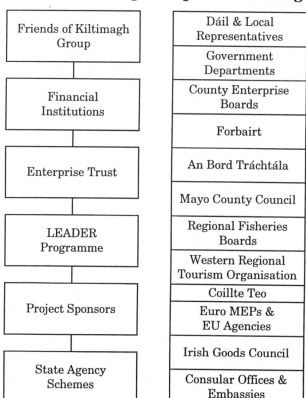

Friends of Kiltimagh
Group

Financial
Institutions

Enterprise Trust

LEADER
Programme

Project Sponsors

State Agency
Schemes

Dáil & Local
Representatives

Government
Departments

County Enterprise
Boards

Forbairt

An Bord Tráchtála

Mayo County Council

Regional Fisheries
Boards

Western Regional
Tourism Organisation

Coillte Teo

Euro MEPs &
EU Agencies

Irish Goods Council

Consular Offices &
Embassies

RTC Galway

RTC Sligo

Teagasc

FÁS

Area
Partnership
Company

Macra
na Feirme

UCD

University
College
Maynooth

Awards (1991–94)

On 28 September 1991, President Mary Robinson presented the company with a cheque for £50,000, as outright winner in the 1991 ESB Community Enterprise Awards. The award was in recognition of the comprehensive development plan prepared by myself as General Manager of the company.

Kiltimagh's was one of 91 such plans submitted by community groups throughout Ireland. Earlier in the year, the plan had been judged as being one of seven category award winners and awarded a prize of £10,000 in the same competition.

In October 1993, the Chairman of IRD Kiltimagh Limited, Mr Brian Mooney, was nominated by Rehab as one of its selections for "Mayo Person of the Year" in recognition of his contribution towards the development of Kiltimagh community.

In September 1994, the town was placed second to Cork City in the Irish Planning Institute Annual Award for Planning, in recognition of the planned changes to the Kiltimagh townscape.

In October 1994, the company was the National Winner of the *Irish Farmers Journal*/Bank of Ireland Community Enterprise Award and received a cheque for £10,000.

Planning Review (1994)

The company undertook a full review of its four-year programme and commenced a new planning phase.

An Tríú Céim (1995–99)

Future plans include a five-year Social Enterprise Programme for the area in conjunction with the Department of Social Welfare. The Social Enterprise Programme will run parallel to the ongoing Business Development Programme started as An Chéad Chéim.

One of the disappointments of the 1990–93 Programme was the failure to stimulate a social enterprise programme, which is recognised as being an essential element of community enterprise. This is now planned for the period 1995–99.

An Cheathrú Céim (1995–99)

This involves a framework within the context of "Kiltimagh —

The Artisan Village" and has three main objectives which are described later.

Involvement with Other Networks

LEADER Programme

Together with North Connaught Farmers Co-operative, Tubbercurry, County Sligo; Moy Valley Resources, Ballina; and Teagasc, the company is one of the constituent parts of Western Rural Development Limited. This company is one of several in Ireland that was assigned by the European Union and the Department of Agriculture to distribute grant assistance to rural development projects in the period 1992–94. IRD Kiltimagh Limited's office is one of two administration offices of the LEADER company and is responsible for an area in East Mayo/South-West Sligo. Western Rural Development Limited was also successful in its application to administer the LEADER II Programme.

Area-Based Partnership

IRD Kiltimagh Limited has two nominees on the board of the Area-Based Partnership (Meitheal Mhaigh Eo). The other representatives are from community-based organisations in Erris, Ballina and Castlebar, along with nominees of the social partners. The initiative was undertaken under the Programme for Economic and Social Progress (PESP) and continued under the Operational Programme for Local, Urban and Rural Development. Its primary objective is the relief of long-term unemployment.

External Partnerships

IRD Kiltimagh Limited has built partnerships with:

(i)   EU Community Initiatives, as part of the EU Community Initiatives Programme, with Menter Powys, Wales

(ii)   "Friends of Kiltimagh" Associations in Dublin, London, New York, New Jersey and Boston.

Characteristics

The general characteristics of the company can be summarised as follows:

(i)   It aims to create permanent jobs and to become self-sufficient in the long term.

(ii)   It was started and is maintained by partnership between public-sector and private companies as well as committed groups and individuals.

(iii)   It is community-based and controlled.

(iv)   All profits or surpluses are directed towards social and community benefit rather than private gain.

11
The Company Prospectus

IRD Kiltimagh Limited launched its Company Prospectus — the document that invited the community to subscribe funds — on 19 July 1989 — in advance of my appointment as general manager. A brief and restrained document that contained a wish-list of what might be possible, it symbolised a community taking its first tentative steps to come to terms with its economic development needs. It combined a series of programmes with suggestions for specific projects. Key parts of the Prospectus read as follows:

Objectives of the Company

The overall long-term objective of IRD Kiltimagh Limited is to develop the economic potential of Kiltimagh and its environs to the fullest, and in a way that will benefit the whole local community. All its more immediate objectives serve this one.

The immediate objectives are:

1. To create a business climate and framework within which local investment in new local enterprise is encouraged and facilitated

2. To identify areas where economic development might take place, be it in the sphere of manufacturing industry and commerce, tourism and entertainment or enterprises based on natural resources

3. To encourage and support promising projects set up to exploit the potential which these spheres of development have to offer

4. To act as a representative body on behalf of the community in negotiating with groups or individuals interested in setting up such enterprises locally

5. Where helpful, to act as "broker" with financial institutions and state agencies on behalf of small enterprises in the matter of arranging funding for project start-up

6. To help small enterprises in the area of management, marketing and further development through the services of the Manager employed by IRD Kiltimagh Limited

7.   To invest some of the company's own funds in worthwhile projects
        where shortage of venture capital is an obstacle to getting started

8.   To invest in the provision of development facilities i.e. office, factory
        space, plant or sites where the attraction of some enterprise or group
        of enterprises seems to warrant it

9.   To help develop the infrastructure of Kiltimagh and the surrounding
        area in a planned way

10.   In the long term, to attract in at least one large outside industry that
        would have a substantial spin-off effect on the whole local economy.

Principles of Operation

Having outlined a number of ways in which IRD Kiltimagh Limited might
help promote economic development in the locality, there are some important
points that need to be made with regard to its mode of operation. While it is
impossible at this stage to give full details of all conditions attaching to the
company's involvement with new enterprises in the area, it is proposed that
all its activities would be governed by the following principles:

1.   All loans and shareholdings undertaken by IRD Kiltimagh Limited
        would be on an arms-length basis where normal commercial criteria
        would apply in examining the suitability and viability of projects.
        Applications for loans/share capital would be vetted by an independ-
        ent committee and their decisions in all cases would be final.

2.   Where a shareholding is taken in a company, IRD Kiltimagh Limited
        would insist on having board representation in keeping with the level
        of investment in that company.

3.   IRD Kiltimagh Limited as a matter of principle would seek to sell its
        investment in individual companies at a commercial profit after a
        limited number of years so that the funds would be available to help
        other projects.

4.   IRD Kiltimagh Limited would probably not make an investment of
        more than 30 per cent of its resources in any one project.

5.   Preference will be given by IRD Kiltimagh Limited to entrepreneurs
        who can demonstrate an ability and willingness to employ people from
        the Kiltimagh area.

6.   The owners and managers of all companies helped by IRD Kiltimagh
        Limited would be encouraged to live in the Kiltimagh area.

7.   IRD Kiltimagh Limited would at all times keep in mind that it is not
        its own money but money subscribed and donated by the people of
        Kiltimagh that is being invested or loaned. It would be its intention
        therefore to take every possible precaution and be guided by the best
        possible advice in using it for the good of the community. However, it is
        important that everyone realises in advance that in the business
        world some failure is inevitable. It would be too much to expect that

everything that is tried is going to succeed. But following the above criteria we are confident that we have the basis for a good development company which over a number of years can greatly improve the local economy, provided it gets the full support of the Kiltimagh community.

The Prospectus

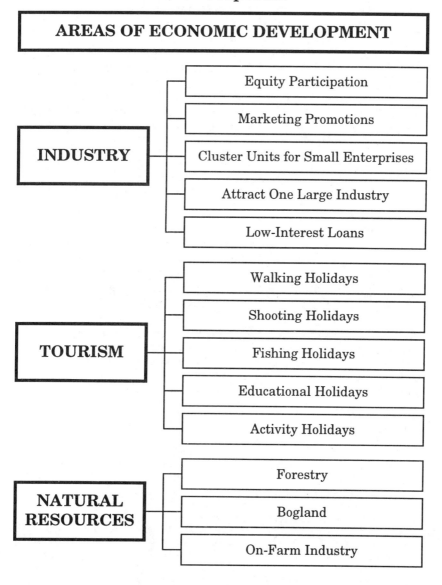

AREAS OF ECONOMIC DEVELOPMENT

INDUSTRY
- Equity Participation
- Marketing Promotions
- Cluster Units for Small Enterprises
- Attract One Large Industry
- Low-Interest Loans

TOURISM
- Walking Holidays
- Shooting Holidays
- Fishing Holidays
- Educational Holidays
- Activity Holidays

NATURAL RESOURCES
- Forestry
- Bogland
- On-Farm Industry

Areas of Economic Development

The areas of economic development the company would hope to explore can be summarised under three headings. They are Industry, Tourism and Natural Resources.

Industry

The attraction of industry to the Kiltimagh area is a central goal in the programme for economic and social regeneration being proposed by IRD Kiltimagh Limited. It sees industrial development as a major key in revitalising the town. If enough industrial jobs can be created, the level of forced emigration will be reduced, families will be kept together, retail businesses will survive and new ones will open. Furthermore, infrastructural development would take place and, not least, a new sense of pride and hope would be instilled in the community. In short, the fabric of our society, in the persons of young people staying at home, marrying and raising their families in the environment in which they themselves were raised, will be kept together. We cannot rely on others to achieve this for us. We must set about achieving it for ourselves.

In particular, it would be a mistake to think that Knock Airport will solve all our economic problems. The presence of the airport so near is certainly a plus factor that can be used to advantage. However, significant local economic development can only take place through initiatives taken within the local community. No one is going to give us jobs. Politicians, the IDA and others, are inundated by special pleas from all sides for special consideration. Given that the number of outside manufacturing companies prepared to invest in Ireland is diminishing, there are great limitations to what we can expect from the IDA. We can seek their help certainly but only when we have done something ourselves.

One of the main functions of IRD Kiltimagh Limited would be to provide a vehicle through which the whole community can work together to initiate industrial development itself. The methods of attracting industry to the area through the company would be varied. It would depend on the resources available to the company and the type of industry being attracted.

Suggested Action to be Taken

1. Liaise with the activities of IDA and Mayo County Development Team to attract industry to the area.

2. Channel BES funds into new and existing businesses.

3. Highlight the potential of the local labour force.

4. Make business community aware of grants and services available from FÁS etc.

5. Provide cluster units for development of small enterprises.

6. Provide centralised office facilities to small businesses and also access

to professional personnel such as accountants and solicitors.

7. Provide, if possible, low-interest loans in start-up situations.

8. Take equity in suitable business ventures.

9. Monitor progress of projects assisted by the company.

10. Arrange marketing and sales promotions for local small industry.

11. Assist in every possible way the location of large industry in the town.

Tourism

One of the key areas earmarked for expansion nationally at the present time is tourism. Substantial funding from both state agencies and the EU is being made available for development in this area. It is the intention of IRD Kiltimagh Limited, in liaison with the local Tourism Association, to explore how Kiltimagh can derive maximum benefit from this industry. The natural amenities the area has to offer, coupled with the nearness of the airport, prompt the company to set as its immediate objective in this sphere the promotion of package holidays selling what the surrounding countryside and other areas within easy reach of Kiltimagh have to interest different kinds of tourist — for example:

- Walking Holidays: Very large numbers of people in Europe are interested in walking. One idea would be to put together a holiday package offering a variety of road and cross-country walking routes. The Kiltimagh area provides the possibility of setting up several such routes. This could be supplemented with a number of day trips to suitable walking districts in other places in Mayo.

- Shooting Holidays: The terrain in the surrounding district provides excellent potential for shooting game. Birds could be bred specially for release and shooting holidays advertised. The local shooting club could have an important role in the organisation of this.

- Fishing Holidays: Local lakes and rivers could be developed especially for coarse fishing. Again other fishing areas a bit further afield could be included as part of the holiday package.

- Educational Holidays: The idea here would be to organise package holidays aimed at a Continental market that would combine the learning of English and recreational activities. This would entail laying on English classes for part of the day and then organising tours, sport and leisure activities for the rest of the time.

- Activities Holidays: An alternative to this would be an activities holiday on its own where the purpose would be solely recreational. This would involve putting together a week of sports and leisure events and competitions based on facilities already there e.g. squash, handball, snooker, pitch and putt, football, swimming (Claremorris) with perhaps cross-country and hill walks mentioned above included.

Suggested Action to be Taken

1. Put together suitable holiday packages to take advantage of the amenities in the area.

2. Encourage agri-tourism and assist individuals with their development plans for same.

3. Produce professional brochure promoting the area.

4. Set up tourist information point in the town.

5. Seek Business Expansion Scheme funding for suitable tourism projects in the area.

6. Liaise with Regional Tourism Organisation and Bord Fáilte.

7. Support efforts to develop amenities in the town.

8. Consult with Mayo County Council on amenity schemes for the area.

9. Professionally market the area at home and overseas.

10. Seek the assistance of Mayo County Council in signposting sites of interest.

11. Examine the possibility of basing some tourist activity around the life of Raftery.

Natural Resources

Kiltimagh Development Company would also have as one of its aims development related to the natural resources of the area. While the tourism section already partly deals with this topic, there are a number of possibilities specifically related to land use not covered there. In particular, these would take in the whole area of agriculture, horticulture, forestry and peat production.

In the main, farming in the area can be divided into three categories: agricultural — dairying; agricultural — mixed; part-time farmers with off-farm income. The first two categories mentioned are, for the most part, the bigger farms which have become increasingly intensive in their land use. Here, winter housing is one of the main innovations in recent years. With so much poor land and so many small farms in the area, not surprisingly part-time farmers make up a big percentage of the total. In keeping with national trends, this type of farming is on the increase. Most off-farm income comes from service industry, building construction and work with the local authorities. But this kind of employment is not in sufficient supply to give a satisfactory living to every part-time farmer.

The result is that, because of the ever-increasing difficulty of making a living on small holdings of land, the farming population continues to decline. IRD Kiltimagh Limited therefore would see it as a priority to assist any new viable ventures directed towards supplementing the income of the farming community. While nothing could be undertaken without much further research, the following are some possibilities the company would see as worth exploring:

- Forestry: There is an increasing amount of timber in the mid-Mayo area now reaching maturity. A project centred round the felling and preparation of this for commercial use might be one possibility. This area is not fully developed at the moment. There are some saw mills around but they mostly produce only very rough timbers. There are very few marketable products produced. There could be a link-up here with the use of finished timber in some project in the small industries sector. With so much land in the locality unfit or marginal in its usefulness for agriculture, further afforestation is another venture that could be undertaken as a long-term investment. While the big returns from this would be very much in the future, it would involve some employment in the planting, growing and thinning of trees. It also would enhance the area from a tourist point of view. For instance, in regard to the walking routes mentioned for tourists, the forests already growing in the locality provide many interesting possibilities.

- On-Farm Industries: The company would encourage on-farm enterprises to supplement farm incomes. Areas such as fruit, flower and vegetable growing might be examined. Production of poultry, deer, rabbits etc. might also be considered if proven feasible.

- Bogland: The area has no scarcity of bog. At present this is being used solely for the purpose of providing home fuel. One possibility here might be a small industry producing milled peat, presuming, of course, that a reliable market outlet can be found.

Suggested Action to be Taken

1. Carry out study of land in surrounding hinterland to ascertain land potential and categorise its value.

2. Seek the help of Teagasc to evaluate the potential of the area for all types of food production.

3. Investigate the potential of alternative farming projects, e.g. organic farming.

4. Evaluate, with the help of Coillte, the potential of existing mature forestry with a view to using same in manufacturing outlet.

5. Work out with the same body a plan for further afforestation and re-afforestation.

6. Evaluate the potential of bogland in the area.

7. Compile information on all forms of commercial peat production with a view to finding a viable product that might suit the Kiltimagh area.

Professional Management

A full-time manager with initiative and a good understanding of business development, competent in marketing, and with considerable selling skills will be recruited. He will be supported by an office and secretary, and will be responsible for identifying and assessing projects, researching them, and reporting to the board. He will be required to encourage and assist the various projects in every way possible. He will be able to call on the specialist skills of the board members. He will develop a viable financial control system for each project. He will market the area at home and abroad. Any product, whether a package holiday or a food product, can only succeed if properly marketed. Numerous reports have alluded to neglect in this domain in Ireland. It is intended therefore that the company will ensure proper marketing of local products through the qualifications of its manager, and by assessing a marketing strategy for its projects at the outset.

Funding

For a number of years the company will depend heavily on voluntary subscriptions. It is hoped that every wage earner will contribute to the company fund, with much more substantial contributions coming from businesses in the area in proportion to the size of their enterprises. It is also hoped that many local clubs and organisations will make a contribution and that natives of the area now abroad will be interested in supporting the efforts of the company either through financial help or with ideas for setting up enterprises. The target being set for voluntary subscriptions to the company development fund is £35,000 per year. To achieve anything worthwhile, it is calculated that the community would need to be prepared to raise this sum.

One of the attractions of the company is that directly raised funds may attract additional finance from Central Government Departments and Agencies, the European Union (EU Structural Funds) and the Irish Resource Trust.

The company will be run along strictly business lines, in keeping with normal procedures in private companies. The aim is to make its subscription money "work" and produce a profit in the course of helping local enterprises. It is hoped that in this way the company will eventually become self-financing and no longer dependent on voluntary subscriptions. However, no profits made will, at any stage, directly benefit any group or individual associated with the company. All such profits will be re-invested in further enterprises undertaken for the good of the local community.

Making it Happen: An Impassioned Plea

The task being undertaken is a daunting one. To achieve success, we rely on what in the end is Kiltimagh's greatest resource — its people and their community spirit. In this regard, we have every cause for confidence. We have an upcoming generation that compares favourably with its peers. The same survey that indicated such high levels of emigration among the youth from the Kiltimagh area has also shown that their level of educational achievement was away above the national average. Ninety per cent of the girls and two-thirds of the boys sat for the Leaving Certificate. Overall 60 per cent went on to further education of at least one year's duration, 40 per cent went to courses of two years or more, and 30 per cent went to university, higher technical colleges or regional colleges. Another 10 per cent went into nursing or apprenticeships.

Among the more adult population, a big plus factor is their remarkable level of community activity in the social and recreational sphere. For a town of its size, Kiltimagh has an extraordinary number of active and competently run community-minded voluntary organisations and groupings. This is indicative of a strong community spirit and an ability to achieve things together. Coupled with the quality of the young labour force the area is producing, it provides a very promising springboard from which to launch a new initiative to revitalise the business life of the town and increase employment in the area. However, to achieve this, the community needs to focus much of its energy and effort on a new goal — namely economic development. The starting point for this is self-belief that we can do something to help ourselves, not only in social and recreational spheres but also in the matter of generating wealth, enterprise and employment in the locality. After that, it is a question of concerted thought and action in making it happen. IRD Kiltimagh Limited provides a suitable structure through which we can harness and channel our efforts in an efficient and co-ordinated way, in the pursuit of this goal together.

In the aftermath of *The Irish Times* articles highlighting the effects of emigration in Kiltimagh, there was a cry that "something must be done" voiced many times in the community. IRD Kiltimagh Limited is an attempt to respond to that cry. Based on the latest thinking about the promotion of local enterprise, it gives us a new opportunity to change the situation. But it is only people who can make it work. It calls for the generous support of the whole community if it is to have any hope of success. A future in Kiltimagh for many families, and especially many of our youth, may depend on it. Give it full-hearted backing and it could mark a great turning point in the business life of the town. If nothing happens and things drift on the way they are, the prospects are bleak. Business will continue to decline and the population to dwindle. Yes, "something must be done!" No one will do it for us. We must do it for ourselves! Let us work to achieve this together through IRD Kiltimagh Limited.

12

The Strategic Community Enterprise Plan:

An Chéad Chéim
(The First Step)
(1991–93)

One year after my appointment, board members were introduced to a series of action plans that had evolved from the Company Prospectus and soundings with the public and the support networks.

The planning process evolved as follows:

An Evolving Planning Process

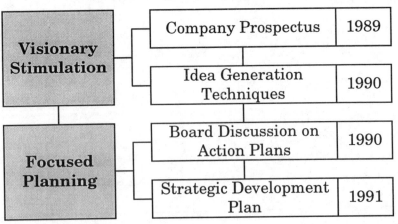

Visionary Stimulation	Company Prospectus	1989
	Idea Generation Techniques	1990
Focused Planning	Board Discussion on Action Plans	1990
	Strategic Development Plan	1991

An Evolving Development Action Plan

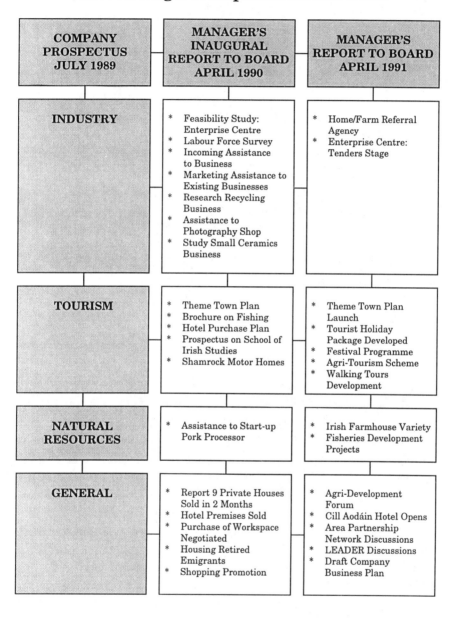

COMPANY PROSPECTUS JULY 1989	MANAGER'S INAUGURAL REPORT TO BOARD APRIL 1990	MANAGER'S REPORT TO BOARD APRIL 1991
INDUSTRY	* Feasibility Study: Enterprise Centre * Labour Force Survey * Incoming Assistance to Business * Marketing Assistance to Existing Businesses * Research Recycling Business * Assistance to Photography Shop * Study Small Ceramics Business	* Home/Farm Referral Agency * Enterprise Centre: Tenders Stage
TOURISM	* Theme Town Plan * Brochure on Fishing * Hotel Purchase Plan * Prospectus on School of Irish Studies * Shamrock Motor Homes	* Theme Town Plan Launch * Tourist Holiday Package Developed * Festival Programme * Agri-Tourism Scheme * Walking Tours Development
NATURAL RESOURCES	* Assistance to Start-up Pork Processor	* Irish Farmhouse Variety * Fisheries Development Projects
GENERAL	* Report 9 Private Houses Sold in 2 Months * Hotel Premises Sold * Purchase of Workspace Negotiated * Housing Retired Emigrants * Shopping Promotion	* Agri-Development Forum * Cill Aodáin Hotel Opens * Area Partnership Network Discussions * LEADER Discussions * Draft Company Business Plan

The Company Business Plan for Development was launched in April 1991 and contained three sections:

IRD Kiltimagh Limited
An Chéad Chéim
Economic Development Programme 1991–93

Section 1	Section 2	Section 3
Socioeconomic Programme	Company Business Projects	Venture Capital Projects

The plan was submitted as an entry in the Community Enterprise Awards Competition, organised by Macra na Feirme and sponsored by the ESB. It secured a prize of £10,000 as a category award winner and later was judged the overall winner of the grand prize of £50,000. On 28 September 1991, President Mary Robinson presented the National Award to IRD Kiltimagh Limited, noting the assessors' statement:

> Kiltimagh's Integrated Development Plan will undoubtedly contribute to a much-needed rejuvenation of the area.

Section 1: Socioeconomic Programme

This contained six "areas of focus", each of which was under the guidance of a voluntary working group leader. Each programme had to advance self-sustaining projects. It was recognised that many aspects of this programme would be costly on local resources and would return no direct monetary benefit. However, each of these was regarded as essential for the improvement of the environmental resources of Kiltimagh town and district. The company recognised the need to create a pleasant environment in which other features of economic development could be progressed.

The goals to be achieved within each programme are outlined below in reports commissioned as part of the 1994 Planning Review. In most cases, the achievements have gone beyond the desired goals.

Socioeconomic Programme — Voluntary Sector

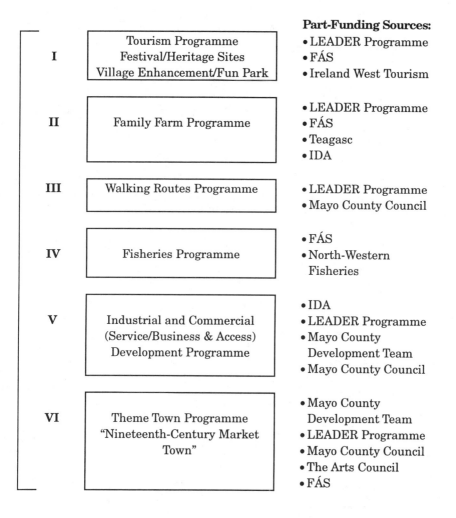

Part-Funding Sources:

I	Tourism Programme Festival/Heritage Sites Village Enhancement/Fun Park	• LEADER Programme • FÁS • Ireland West Tourism
II	Family Farm Programme	• LEADER Programme • FÁS • Teagasc • IDA
III	Walking Routes Programme	• LEADER Programme • Mayo County Council
IV	Fisheries Programme	• FÁS • North-Western Fisheries
V	Industrial and Commercial (Service/Business & Access) Development Programme	• IDA • LEADER Programme • Mayo County Development Team • Mayo County Council
VI	Theme Town Programme "Nineteenth-Century Market Town"	• Mayo County Development Team • LEADER Programme • Mayo County Council • The Arts Council • FÁS

Tourism Programme Report

Working Group Leader: Francis McNicholas

Goals:

(i)   To assist with the continuation of the highly successful St Patrick's Week Festival.

Report: Goal achieved. The St Patrick's Week Festival is now an "off-season" international event. The Quaker City String Band from Philadelphia, with an entourage of 100, has returned every year since 1987. The German Banner-Waving Group, Fanfarenzug Niederburg Konstanz, has attended each year since 1993. In 1993, the parade theme

"A Pageant of Mayo History" involved Galway arts group, Macnas, in the development of floats and accessories. The festival is now one of the highlights of Mayo's and Ireland's entertainment calendar.

In this regard, the work begun by Nancy Shannon, Judy Byrne, Nuala Higgins, Helen Tarpey, Mary Carney and Gerry Walsh was complemented by the massive effort of others, with particular inputs from Francis McNicholas and Brendan Killeen.

(ii)   To revive the traditional August Fair.

Report: Goal achieved. The Committee organised "An Béal Oscailte", a folk/story-telling festival in keeping with the Kiltimagh association with the blind nineteenth-century poet, Raftery of Cill Aodáin.

(iii)   To enhance the presentation of the town and district of Kiltimagh and to assist with the Tidy Towns Competition.

Report: Considerable advancement by private businesses in keeping with the Theme Town programme. Some poorly presented sites are still detracting from this effort.

(iv)   To encourage entertainment for visitors with emphasis on the traditional.

Report: The pubs have adapted well to assisting with this effort and gradually the popularity of traditional entertainment is evolving. In April 1993, the company organised the Irish première of Patrick Cassidy's cantata, *The Children of Lir*. The event was staged in the Church of the Holy Family and was a gala occasion. The London-based Tallis Chamber Choir was flown into Knock International Airport, courtesy of Ryan Air. The RTE Concert Orchestra performance gave the sense of traditional an impetus, which will have a lasting effect. Other festival developments also add to the community sense of the traditional. In a separate development, traditional street theatre is gradually evolving as a popular attraction. A bilingual programme for the improvement in the use of the Irish language is being supported by Bord na Gaeilge.

Note 1:   The development of a Heritage Trail is underway. Compiled with Kiltimagh Historical Society in conjunction with Boston businessman and former Kiltimagh native, Mr Tom Flatley, the trail continues to improve facilities at the Railway Museum. Other Developments on the Heritage Trail include: Cill Aodáin monastic site; the Town Forge/Museum; Ballinamore Church of Ireland site; access to Mooney's Ring Fort; Cultrasna Penal Village; the development of a picnic site; erection of signs for tourist information at relevant points; the Old Schoolhouse Museum.

Note 2:   The development of a Venture Fun Park with assistance from Ireland West Tourism on the two-acre Well Boreen Site is a unique project for Mayo providing natural playground amenities and is an excellent facility for local children and visitors alike.

Family Farm Programme Report

Working Group Leader: Anthony McNicholas

Goals:

(i)   To establish courses and co-ordination in food production and alternative farm enterprises in order to provide supplementary income.

Report: During Autumn 1991/Spring 1992, a FÁS/Teagasc course for farm-fresh food producers was held in the John A. McNiece Training Centre. The 26 participants were trained in business methods and received certificates in food hygiene.

(ii)   To provide off-farm supplementary income for farmers/families by other projects and programmes.

Report: Ongoing and accelerating opportunities within the EU LEADER programme. The LEADER programme can facilitate and assist any farmer in the locality who has an idea for developing projects in the food sector to provide full-time or supplementary income, provided that such projects do not involve production of products that are already over-supplied on the market. Some examples of assisted developments within the LEADER Programme include: a farm-fresh poultry producer; a traditional farmhouse bakery; an organic vegetable producer; a traditional-cure pork/bacon producer; a study of primary processing facilities; a snail-farming study.

(iii)   To stimulate, establish and market an effective Rural Tourism Project.

Report: Within the LEADER programme, accommodation providers are encouraged and assisted in the refurbishment of derelict cottages for self-catering accommodation and in the provision of en-suite facilities in existing Bed and Breakfasts. Management at IRD Kiltimagh Limited has co-ordinated groups from surrounding towns and villages that have produced a full-colour brochure (with the assistance of Ireland West Tourism) of the region, now known as "Celtic Mayo".

(iv)   To work with Teagasc Advisory Services and the state agencies to encourage alternative enterprises.

Report: Ongoing meetings and projects examined while working with local groups and individuals.

(v)   To organise a series of regional fora on problems in the agri-sector.

Report: In May 1991, the first such conference was held, attended by many state and farming officials and by EU Commissioner, Mr Ray McSharry. The official report from this conference was presented to all relevant bodies and some of its recommendations — particularly relating to small farmers' dole and the freezing of assessment to allow for development — are now being adopted by the relevant authorities. A second forum, entitled "Looking up for Jobs" was held in October 1992. This was addressed by Mary O'Rourke, TD, Minister for Trade and Marketing. These fora were sponsored by NCF Co-op and the ESB respectively.

(vi)   To study the possibility of establishing a small food-processing centre for farm-fresh produce.

Report: The IDA-assisted study has been prepared, leading to the conclusion that the provision of a central processing facility for 5,000 farm-fresh birds per week is feasible.

(vii)   To co-ordinate progress on fresh-food production and marketing.

Report: Refer to Irish Farmhouse Variety Limited Report.

Note 1: Rural Resettlement Ireland Limited: As an additional effort to alleviate the worst effects of depopulation, IRD Kiltimagh Limited has embarked upon a networking programme with Rural Resettlement Ireland Limited which is based in County Clare. The office works closely with Rural Resettlement Ireland and many houses have been sourced, which will soon be occupied by families from the cities. Twelve families have been settled throughout County Mayo. Work is ongoing to source as many houses as possible, particularly in the Kiltimagh area.

Walking Routes Report

Working Group Leader: Michael O'Sullivan

Goal:
(i)   By the end of Year 2, to provide a series of walking routes for visitors.

Report: The project is completed and seven routes have been sign-posted around country lanes and to the summit of Sliabh Chairn. Detailed maps for walkers have been provided with the assistance of the LEADER programme. Ongoing discussions are taking place with Mayo County Council and Cospóir in order to have an extension of the Mayo-Western Way to include walks on Sliabh Chairn.

Fisheries Report

Working Group Leader: Brendan Killeen

Goals:
(i)   To have the name of Kiltimagh associated with game angling and coarse fishing.

Report: A Kiltimagh Angling Club was formed to co-ordinate this. Over the past two years, various groups visited the area from France and the UK in order to fish the Moy and Gweestion rivers and local lakes. Signposting has been erected to indicate the direction of the rivers Moy and Gweestion from the centre of Kiltimagh town. The National Pike Fishing Competition was hosted by Kiltimagh Angling Club in 1995.

(ii)   To provide good services and facilities for fishermen.

Report: The development of the Cill Aodáin Hotel and further Bed and Breakfast accommodation have helped here. More work needs to be done on: (a) providing tackle and drying rooms for anglers, and (b) the organisation of a festival with fishing/angling as a central theme.

(iii) To develop facilities on the Pollagh and Glore Rivers.

Report: The North-Western Fisheries Board organised a FÁS Scheme and, as a result, access has been improved, stiles erected, and overhanging gorse and shrubs removed. A recent Central Fisheries Board Report on the River Pollagh indicated the possibility of approximately 1,000 fresh brown trout per mile of water. Conservation of fishing stocks is an urgent priority.

(iv) To support an action plan for the co-ordinated development of the Moy Fisheries.

Report: Full support has been given and submissions to the plan were made.

(v) To work with the Fisheries Board to develop access to local lakes for coarse fishing.

Report: An initial report has been received and discussed by Kiltimagh Angling Club.

(vi) To request relevant agencies to organise a training course for ghillies.

Report: Little progress to date.

Industrial and Commercial Services / Business and Access Development Report

Industrial Development

Goals:

(i) To attract a number of small firms to locate either in the Community Enterprise Centre or elsewhere in Kiltimagh.

Report: See Enterprise House Report.

(ii) In the long term, to seek to attract a large data-processing unit to Kiltimagh.

Report: Brochure launched on potential for Data-Processing Development from Kiltimagh. This brochure was sponsored by Tom Flatley, Boston. Efforts to attract investors in such an industry are continuing.

Commercial Infrastructure

Working Group Leaders: Ann-Marie Carroll and Brenda McNicholas

Goals:

(i) To make Kiltimagh a complete self-contained retail shopping unit.

Report: Many new shops have opened and, through very hard lobbying, a shoe shop has once again opened in the town. The provision of the excellent Cill Aodáin Hotel was a welcome investment as an additional and essential piece of infrastructure in a small town like Kiltimagh.

(ii) To influence behavioural attitudes of local people to shopping in Kiltimagh.

Report: The twelve months shopping promotion which finished in June 1991 was an effort to achieve some changes in attitude. A concurrent promotion/awareness campaign in the schools also helped.

The shopping promotion prizes cost £15,000 and many of these were sponsored by firms doing business in the town. It is hoped that more people are now aware of shopping locally to help keep jobs at home.

The company has now undertaken to organise a network campaign, CUT (Communities Under Threat), the objective of which is to increase awareness of spending locally so as to create a spin-off multiplier effect. This campaign is co-ordinated by IRD Kiltimagh Limited for the entire of County Mayo. In recent months, the campaign has been launched in other counties and has attracted much media attention at national level. The campaign is now supported by one large grocery-wholesaling firm.

Services Infrastructure

Goal:

(i)   To ensure the availability and viability of essential services.

Report: Through continuous political lobbying, we are happy to report that the Western Health Board now offers a range of services and facilities in the new Health Centre (at the former Primary School). Discussions are ongoing with the Western Health Board regarding additional services. Other community services are also on offer from Enterprise House and at other locations. Queries are dealt with on a regular basis and much needs to be done to protect and support existing services while also attracting new services. The provision of excellent hotel facilities at the Cill Aodáin Hotel is a real boost for the town.

Approach Roads

Goals:

(i)   To make Kiltimagh more accessible by virtue of better approach roads.

Report: The removal of the bottlenecks at the railway gates on two approaches has helped. Mayo County Council is to prepare a report on the narrow bridge at Annaghill. The new roads plan provides for traffic from Ballina to Galway to be routed from Bohola (N5) via Kiltimagh to Knock (N17). A FÁS scheme is working on improving the appearance of approach roads and the back-streets of the town.

(ii)   To keep constant pressure on relevant authorities for funding improvements.

Report: Regular informal and formal meetings are held with public representatives and with county officials to ensure that a fair share of the tight budget for improvements comes to the area. The provision of overhead traffic-route lighting has brightened the appearance of the town. Compulsory purchase of some derelict sites is also proceeding.

Theme Town Report

Working Group Leader: Brian Mooney

Goals:

(i)   That the Kiltimagh townscape will gradually, over the next four years, begin to reflect the theme "A nineteenth-century market town".

Photo 1: First Day at the Office — *(L to R)* Padraic Brennan (Board Member), Pat Dillon (Board Member), John Higgins and Siobhan Gorman (UK Travel Agent).

Photo 2: Visit to "Friends of Kiltimagh", Boston, February 1993 — *(L to R Foregound)* Tom McNicholas, Tom Flatley, John Higgins and Tom Meenaghan.

Photo 3: The ESB Community Enterprise Awards, July 1993 — (L to R) John Higgins, Peadar Healy (ESB Sligo), Brian Mooney, Sadie Mulhern and Padraic Brennan.

Photo 4: The Sculpture Park and Museum, with Raifteirí an File centre, completed September 1993.

Photo 5: Visit of Aosdána to Kiltimagh, October 1993 — *(L to R Standing)* Brendan Killeen, Dermot Healy, Joe Kelly, David Shaw Smith, Tom Kilroy, Camille Sutre, Bob Quinn, Paul Durcan, Bernard Farrell. *(L to R Seated)* Adrian Munnelly (Director, Arts Council), Mary Fitzgerald, Imogen Stuart and Ulick O'Connor.

Photo 6: Some Leaders of Project Working Groups, June 1994 — (*L to R Standing*) Anthony McNicholas, Joe Kelly, Pat Dillon, Nancy Lavin, Brian Mooney, Betty Solan, John Higgins, Brendan Killeen, Don Dillon. (*L to R Seated*) Sadie Mulhern, Brenda McNicholas, Regina Higgins, Mary Glynn, Joan Tarpey, Bridie McMahon, Ann McNicholas, Claire Hickey.

Photo 7: President Robinson in Kiltimagh, July 1994 — (*L to R*) Nick Robinson, President Mary Robinson, John Higgins and Brendan Killeen (Board Member).

Photo 8: Enterprise House, Aiden Street, Kiltimagh, with IRD Kiltimagh offices on left, July 1994.

(ii)   That the theme will distinguish Kiltimagh from other Irish towns.

(iii)   That this will be a "cause célèbre" for the inhabitants.

(iv)   That this distinctiveness will be a source of attraction to outsiders.

Report: An architectural plan has been prepared for the town. This has been accepted by Mayo County Council as a basis of planning and design. Many shops and businesses have changed to conform with the plan. The area in and around the Market Square has been refurbished according to the plan.

The first piece of sculpture, "An Chéad Chéim" (The First Step), of a planned sculpture trail on approach roads has been located in the Venture Fun Park. The piece was sponsored by The Arts Council of Ireland and the Arts Committee of Mayo County Council. A water-sculpture "Eternal Spring" in the Market Square relieves the harshness of dry stone walls and provides an inspiration for further development.

Traditional lamp-standards have been erected on Main Street. A plan for soft-landscaping and seating has been prepared by the County Architect's Office. Monies for traditional lights on Main Street have been provided by Friends of Kiltimagh in London, by the Irish-American Partnership, Boston and by individual emigrant subscription.

The development of a Theme Village at Cultrasna and the Town Forge on the Well Boreen Site are being advanced. The development by Kiltimagh Historical Society of Killedan Monastery Site was also undertaken with the direct involvement of IRD Kiltimagh Limited. Funding is being matched by EU funding for such projects. Mr Tom Flatley (via the American-Ireland Fund) has assisted with this development.

The provision of paint schemes for householders has been very successful in providing a brighter and more visually attractive town. The development of a "green park" at Main Street adjacent to the O'Hara Home has been discussed with the Western Health Board and will be completed in 1995.

Section 2 — Company Business Plan

Seven projects were chosen which research revealed were economically feasible and capable of becoming self-sustaining. Research also indicated the need for some socially desirable projects to be included in what was essentially an economic development plan. The inclusion of a training centre and housing for the retired elderly were responses to this need. It was also apparent that some projects would be slow to show a return on investment. The job-creating potential in others was obvious — particularly in relation to the provision of an enterprise centre. It was hoped to bring the projects to a point where they would attract either external investment participation or a worker/management buy-out.

Company Business Projects

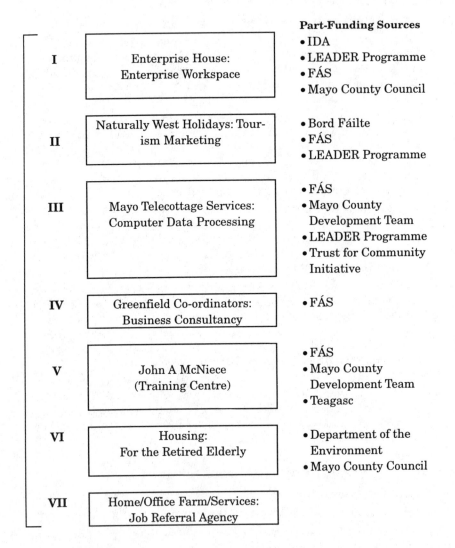

Part-Funding Sources

I — Enterprise House: Enterprise Workspace
- IDA
- LEADER Programme
- FÁS
- Mayo County Council

II — Naturally West Holidays: Tourism Marketing
- Bord Fáilte
- FÁS
- LEADER Programme

III — Mayo Telecottage Services: Computer Data Processing
- FÁS
- Mayo County Development Team
- LEADER Programme
- Trust for Community Initiative

IV — Greenfield Co-ordinators: Business Consultancy
- FÁS

V — John A McNiece (Training Centre)
- FÁS
- Mayo County Development Team
- Teagasc

VI — Housing: For the Retired Elderly
- Department of the Environment
- Mayo County Council

VII — Home/Office Farm/Services: Job Referral Agency

The concept of a "televillage" was uppermost in my mind when these projects were being prepared. This concept involved the creation of a network of essential service businesses that would sell services in the broader marketplace, while also providing a back-up service system for local business enterprise. The projects and their goals are reported on below.

Enterprise House

Manager: Joe Kelly

Direct employment: 31 full-time; 12 part-time

Goals:

(i) With IDA Grant Assistance, to purchase properties in the town and to convert these into small industrial/service units for renting to start-up businesses.

(ii) To meet the existing demand for small units suitable for light manufacturing projects.

(iii) To provide an inducement to locals who may have ideas to start their own manufacturing business but are hindered by lack of readily available space.

(iv) To entice entrepreneurs to Kiltimagh.

(v) To increase numbers employed in small manufacturing work.

(vi) To stem partly the flow of emigration from the locality.

Report: Arising from a Feasibility Study conducted by the General Manager, the purchase of three disused buildings was proceeded with. Enterprise House consists of 1,000 square metres providing 16 units of workspace for the following businesses: IRD Kiltimagh Limited, The Farmhouse Pantry, Kiltimagh Business Bureau, Kiltimagh Stained Glass Studios & Millinery, CMS Peripherals, Greenfield Co-ordinators, Naturally West Holidays, Western Rural Development Company, Reservation and Information Marketing Systems, Mayo Arts Network, John A. McNiece Centre, Knocwirra Jewellery, Tom Byrne and East Mayo Forestry Group. Other firms are awaiting workspace. A FÁS (CYTP) Scheme completed the extension.

Enterprise House has a full-time manager. The official opening of the centre was performed by the President of Ireland, Mary Robinson, on 28 July 1994. Three adjacent and derelict sites have been purchased from Mayo County Council to provide parking space and the opportunity for further extension of workspace. Enterprise House has recently acquired a further 3,200 square metres of workspace at the former Irish Spinners Factory. Four tenants have applied for workspace and the initial projected employment is 20. Forbairt has approved grant-assistance for this. The essential element of self-sustainment ensures that while the buildings are owned by IRD Kiltimagh Limited on behalf of the community subscribers, the workspace is rented to all tenants including the owners in order to create a self-sustaining project.

Naturally West Holidays

Manager: Aisling Cahill

Direct employment: 1 full-time; 1 part-time

Goals:

(i) To provide commissionable fully-inclusive fishing, golfing, language learning, walking and go-as-you-please holidays for incoming tourists.

Report: Initially the marketing title "IRD Kiltimagh Tourism" was adopted, with holiday-package brochures for the fishing, golfing, and walking markets being prepared. Trade fairs and Workshops were attended in Dublin, Belfast and Cork. Bord Fáilte Workshops for the travel trade are attended annually. Marketing promotions to mainland Europe and the UK are undertaken regularly. The French market for language-learning students was accessed in 1991, and every year over 80 students come to Kiltimagh to learn English. It is estimated that this provides a £10,000 plus boost to the local economy.

In 1993, IRD Kiltimagh Tourism adopted a new trade name, "Naturally West Holidays", incorporated as "Mayo Celtic Holidays Limited". This company has full-time management and research assistance. The concentration of marketing effort is on the non-English speaking markets of Europe and for the fishing and golfing holiday markets in particular. The products being sold are the best available from the Atlantic Ocean to the Shannon River.

The company also performs a marketing role for a number of special product providers. It is currently endeavouring to provide a network of good family-run hotels from Cork to Donegal for the go-as-you-please visitor touring the entire West of Ireland.

(ii)   To establish Kiltimagh as a holiday centre with good value for money.

Report: Kiltimagh had already been established as an accommodation base for Knock Shrine pilgrims. The town had 55 approved beds in 1989. The number of approved beds is now 106. The facilities at the Cill Aodáin Hotel, the Raftery Rooms, the new coffee shops and fast-food outlets now place Kiltimagh in a position to capitalise on tourism.

The Kiltimagh Heritage Trail, Sculpture Park, Artists' Retreat, Theatre and Exhibition Centre and Venture Park provide extra additional facilities to provide a critical mass of attractions for those seeking value-for-money holidays.

(iii)   To attract the following numbers of tourists to the area for activity holidays: 1991 — 50; 1992 — 100; 1993 — 150.

Report: The company surpassed the initial targets as indicated.

(iv)   To register eventually as an Incoming Tourism Marketing Agency.

Report: In a more recent development, Naturally West Holidays is negotiating a horizontal merger for a joint tour operator business, selling to the incoming and outgoing tourist trade. An off-shoot business, called Reservation and Information Marketing Systems (RIMS), will soon become the first Regional Marketing System possibly linked to the Bord Fáilte "Gulliver" marketing system. This further aspect of marketing linkage for small producers was devised after the General Manager proposed the idea to some Digital Galway employees shortly after the announcement of the Digital closure. Working through the Enterprise Manager, Joe Kelly, and Luke Moran of Wireless Datacom Networks (which comprises some former Digital employees), a partnership company of IRD Kiltimagh and Wireless and Datacom Networks has commenced operations using an on-line telematically-controlled reservations system working by linkage to the Internet and Gulliver. The system, called RIMS (Reservations and Information Marketing Systems), will provide the only on-line system directly from customer to product provider. The plan is to have a central database (server) in Kiltimagh, with approximately 150 product providers. Once the system has been proof-tested, other servers will be provided for other community-based companies to become involved in servicing their areas. The system will be self-sustaining and will source most of its income from advertisers of local amenities.

Kiltimagh Business Bureau

Manager: Joan Tarpey

Direct employment: 1 full-time

Goals:

(i)   To establish a small services industry in computer data entry and processing.

(ii)   To establish an independent computer advice centre, called Mayo Telecottage Services, which will provide internal/external advice and training to the general public, together with access to relevant data bases.

Report: Initially, business commenced by employing persons on FÁS schemes and providing a computer-printing office-bureau and book-keeping facility for Kiltimagh and for tenants of Enterprise House. In keeping with company policy, this business has been the subject of a worker/management buy-out and is now operating as a private business. Kiltimagh Business Bureau sells all the services required by modern offices, including fax, secretarial services, typesetting, brochure production, photocopies, booklet-binding. The original goals of Mayo Telecottage Services will now be transferred to RIMS and/or Naturally West Access.

Greenfield Co-ordinators Limited

Manager: Mary Keane

Direct employment: 2 full-time; 1 part-time

Goals:

(i)   To provide a facility in professional brokerage for new businesses. This independent company to be capable of giving advice in: (a) business management and marketing; (b) tourism promotion and marketing; (c) community development planning.

Report: The company is another subject of the worker/management buy-out policy of IRD Kiltimagh Limited. The company now provides the following services: Business and Marketing Consultation; Business Planning; Feasibility Studies; Marketing Planning; Preparation and Production of Reports; Completion of Grant Applications; Community Development Training and Planning Facilitation.

John A. McNiece Centre

Direct employment: Nil

Indirect employment: 124 trainees

Goals:

(i)   To provide location and equipment for a training facility in the town.

(ii)   To market the facility to providers of relevant training courses.

(iii)   In conjunction with relevant agencies, to provide training courses for farmers, businesses and tourist-related schemes.

Report: The Training Centre has provided facilities for over 120 trainees who participated in a range of courses such as: farm-fresh food business; traditional crafts business; community enterprise development; landscape painting. The development is being assisted by American-born John A. McNiece (Jnr). Mr McNiece is a well-known business personality in Boston and is closely associated with the American-Ireland Fund, Boston. The centre, which is also used as a Boardroom by IRD Kiltimagh Limited, is dedicated to the honour of its patron.

Housing for Retired Elderly

Working Group Leaders: Pat Dillon and Anne Marie Carroll

Direct employment: Nil

Temporary employment: 10

Goals:

(i)   To purchase a number of derelict buildings/sites in the town and to provide self-contained housing units for persons in need of housing. Total number of units planned: 12.

(ii)   To maintain the houses and environs in a way that will enhance the appearance of the town.

Report: Initially this project was targeted at retired emigrants. Because of restrictions in assistance to Voluntary Housing Groups, imposed by the Department of Environment, it was impossible to proceed as initially planned. The target market was then altered to domestic housing-lists. The "People in Need" Fund gave the initial cash boost of £5,000 to this project. The former Corcoran site, Main Street, was purchased and three units were installed there. The official opening of this scheme was performed by Fr Harry Bohan from County Clare in April 1993. A Social Committee for Tenant Care has now been established. A further eight houses are being built on a site at the rear of Aiden Street. The total cost of the scheme is in excess of £350,000.

Office / Home and Farm Services Agency

Goals:

(i)   To provide a computer data base and a referral agency of services provided by local people for office, home or farm services.

(ii)   To provide increased indirect employment.

(iii)   To generate small annual income for the company.

Report: Initial research indicated difficulties with insurance. No further research has been conducted because of lack of manpower.

Section 3 — Venture Capital Projects

These projects have been assisted by the company through small equity shareholdings and a considerable input in kind by way of planning and operational assistance. Three projects were started. A fourth project — a self-catering complex — was disbanded after planning, because funding was unavailable and it was in conflict with the LEADER programme scheme to renovate derelict houses.

Venture Capital Projects

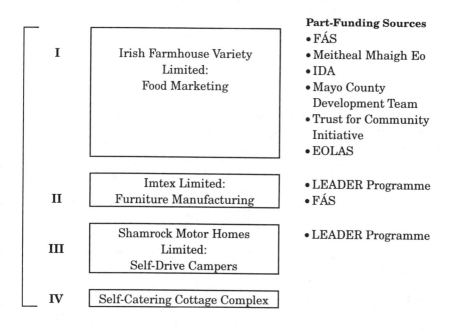

		Part-Funding Sources
I	Irish Farmhouse Variety Limited: Food Marketing	• FÁS • Meitheal Mhaigh Eo • IDA • Mayo County Development Team • Trust for Community Initiative • EOLAS
II	Imtex Limited: Furniture Manufacturing	• LEADER Programme • FÁS
III	Shamrock Motor Homes Limited: Self-Drive Campers	• LEADER Programme
IV	Self-Catering Cottage Complex	

Irish Farmhouse Variety Limited

Managers: Martin Heneghan and Patricia Murphy-Byrne

Direct employment: 3

Indirect employment: 28

In keeping with company policy of initiating and/or supporting marketing-linkage companies for small producers, the original proposer of the business

Irish Farmhouse Variety, Martin Heneghan, was assisted with project development. The company was relocated to Kiltimagh and has operated from Enterprise House since 1992. Its original shareholder base of Mr Heneghan and Golden Vale was expanded to include North Connacht Farmers Co-operative and IRD Kiltimagh Limited. Under new management, seconded by Teagasc, the company adopted the brand-label, "The Farmhouse Pantry". A food-technologist was employed with the assistance of Meitheal Mhaigh Eo and EOLAS. IDA assistance in market research and County Development Team assistance with marketing helped sales to advance steadily. New products were sourced, specific products were given the brand-label and 21 further producers were helped to come on-line. In 1994, the shareholding of the company was rescheduled by agreement. Mr Heneghan's new company assumed the role of distribution agent, with the franchise for certain geographical areas. Ownership of Irish Farmhouse Variety Limited is now in the hands of IRD Kiltimagh Limited and North Connacht Farmers Co-operative. A consultant was employed to prepare a strategic plan for an expanded marketing drive. The company has ceased trading in food produce (the trading aspect now being undertaken by an agent) and is now in the business of developing the brand-label and in franchising this label.

Imtex Limited

Direct employment: 15 full-time (1993), 3 full-time (1994)

Imtex Limited was located in 250 square metres of Enterprise House and employed 15 full-time persons. Its business was the manufacture of high-quality free-standing bedroom furniture. The company directors and shareholders are IRD Kiltimagh Limited together with one of the original proposers and one other. The company made big inroads into the marketplace but ceased trading in 1993.

A further investor with interests in the furniture business became involved, and the new business occupies 750 square metres of the former Irish Spinners Factory. Employment is projected at nine in 1995.

Shamrock Motor Homes Limited

Manager: Pa McNicholas

Direct employment: 1 full-time; 1 part-time

Shamrock Motor Homes Limited is a Camper Hire-Drive company, providing self-drive camper units for the home and incoming tourist trade. This company is owned by J.J. McNicholas Travel, A. Cleary & Sons and IRD Kiltimagh Limited. Bookings during the 1992 season have been excellent. In 1993 and 1994, the company has worked an agency agreement with Cara Motor Homes, Shannon Airport. The company has been appointed as an Irish agent for the British manufacturers Elldis and has begun importing camper bodies for fitting on cabs. These are being sold or used as self-drive stock. Development plans include purchasing more units for self-drive business and the expansion of the sale-of-cabs business.

Self-Catering Cottage Complex

Working Group Leader: Thomas McNicholas

Direct employment: Nil

The aim was to provide eight self-catering cottages on a site at the Forge/ Well Boreen. Planning permission and Bord Fáilte agreement were put in place. With the advent of the LEADER programme scheme for derelict cottages, and because this scheme has seen the refurbishment of a number of cottages in local rural areas, the plan for a complex was abandoned. The site now contains the Venture Fun Park referred to earlier.

13

The Strategic Community Enterprise Plan:

An Dara Céim
(The Second Step)
(1992–95)

In 1992 it became apparent that, while the push for economic development was beginning to have the desired effect, there was a significant section of the local community that was largely unaware of, or apathetic towards, what was happening. I also realised that, while the physical and economical environment was changing for the better, much of what was being done was failing to raise the spirit of the people. Finally, it was evident that, while there was some active creativity, there was a large reserve of latent creativity that could be unleashed in order to counteract the apathy and produce further economic stimuli.

I was asked by members of the Kiltimagh Dramatic Society to produce a project that would help refurbish the Town Hall Theatre, formerly the Newtownbrowne National School. This 300-seat theatre was the property of the Kiltimagh Amateur Dramatic Society, which was over 80 years old and included some significant productions in its "Hall of Fame". Time had taken its toll on the roof and the external structure was rapidly deteriorating.

An Dara Céim

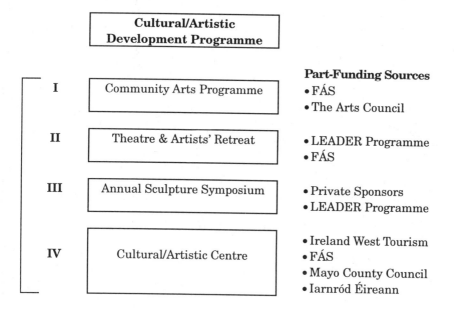

Cultural/Artistic Development Programme	Part-Funding Sources
I — Community Arts Programme	• FÁS • The Arts Council
II — Theatre & Artists' Retreat	• LEADER Programme • FÁS
III — Annual Sculpture Symposium	• Private Sponsors • LEADER Programme
IV — Cultural/Artistic Centre	• Ireland West Tourism • FÁS • Mayo County Council • Iarnród Éireann

For some time, the idea of a Community Arts Project had been, considered by management. Sculptor Jackie McKenna had already produced a magnificent sculpture, "An Chéad Chéim", unveiled in the Market Square by County Manager, Des Mahon.

At a meeting in Dublin between Jackie McKenna and myself to discuss future sculpture development for Kiltimagh, ideas emerged that led to the formulation of the following plan, which now is commonly described as "An Dara Céim" (The Second Step).

An Dara Céim

Community Arts Programme

Working Group Leaders: Thomas McNicholas and Brendan Killeen

Goal: To involve individuals, the community and community groups in multi-forms of art expression.

Report: As a means of self-expression and self-projection, a three-year Community Arts Programme is underway with the aim of developing all art forms including music, poetry, theatre, film and painting. Sculpture as a means of expression has been given significant emphasis. The possibility of further developing the traditional is being studied, with particular emphasis on language, dance, folk-poetry and story-telling.

In order to introduce the community to the excellence of art, the management established contact with two national projects which were co-ordinated by voluntary committees:

Patrick Cassidy's cantata in Irish, *The Children of Lir*, was performed in March 1993 in Kiltimagh parish church. The occasion was a splendid affair, with the RTE Concert Orchestra performing together with the London Tallis Chamber Choir.

In September 1993, IRD Kiltimagh, in conjunction with the Arts Council of Ireland, acted as hosts to the General Assembly of Aosdána. Aosdána is an affiliation of artists, established by An Chomhairle Ealaíon/the Arts Council in 1981, to honour those artists whose work has made an outstanding contribution to the arts in Ireland, and to encourage and assist members in devoting their energies fully to their art. Membership consists of not more than two hundred artists who have distinguished themselves by the excellence of their art. A General Assembly of all Aosdána members is held annually to discuss issues relevant to the status of the artists and the arts in society, and to review the affairs of the organisation. The attendance at the 1993 Assembly consisted of 60 members, who were guests of IRD Kiltimagh. Many artists provided workshops of their productions.

Theatre and Artists' Retreat

Working Group Leaders: Brian Mooney, Chris Glynn and Ann McNicholas

Goal: To refurbish the Town Hall Theatre to provide additional facilities to entice artists to Kiltimagh.

Report: The objective of refurbishing the Town Hall Theatre produced a project to cater for artists-in-residence. Already this facility has been occupied by a number of resident artists/artisans. As an extension of this programme, the former railway station platforms, waiting room, and signal-box have been refurbished and the area cleaned, walled and landscaped to provide an Artists' Retreat Park in the unique ambience of a former railway station.

Sculpture Symposium

Working Group Leader: Don Dillon, Brendan Killeen and Nancy Lavin

Goal: To introduce the community to sculpture as an art form and to produce some fine examples.

Report: The five-week symposium took place in Autumn 1993. Working through the various media of stone, bronze and wood, gradually a beautiful sculpture park appeared on the landscape of the Artists Retreat Park. Seven pieces are now on view in the Sculpture Park. These are:

◊   Taking Flight — in limewood by Jackie McKenna

◊ Reclining Figure — in bathstone by Seamus Dunbar

◊ Raifteirí — in granite by Benedict Byrne

◊ Iníon Mathú — in limestone by Fred Conlon

◊ The Station Master — in bronze by Vincent Brown

◊ Emigration — in limewood by Janet Mullarney

◊ Shibumi — in limestone by Eileen McDonagh.

The Sculpture Trainee programme also produced three pieces. A further water-piece by Benedict Byrne was produced for the Market Square and the "An Chéad Chéim" sculpture was relocated to the Venture Fun Park. Kiltimagh Sculpture Park is now an excellent attractive feature in the town. During the Symposium, 16 local students participated and produced two lovely sculptures under the watchful eye of the experts.

Cultural / Artistic Centre

Working Group Leader: Danny Doherty

Goal: To reconstruct the station master's house as an exhibition centre and workspace for artists.

Report: The former station master's house was in ruins and in a dangerous condition. It was planned to have this project undertaken in 1995. With the assistance of Ireland West Tourism and FÁS, the project commenced in December 1993 and took six weeks to complete. The first exhibition of paintings, by local painter Alan Skelton, took place in March 1993. Regular exhibitions are now held.

Discussions have commenced with The Arts Council on operational schemes for utilisation of all the facilities undertaken under "An Dara Céim".

14
Economic Review

The results of any business plan can only be assessed by a review process. Community enterprise plans are no different from any private commercial business although only rarely is time given to looking back and analysing both the achievements and failures. An acceptance of failure, as well as achievement, is indicative of maturity in both voluntary and professional management. Too often, analysis of community enterprise highlights only the achievements and the physical environmental changes by way of "bricks and mortar" and fails, or fears, to reveal or accept the successes and failures in human resource development.

Jobs

The Achilles heel of community enterprise must always be the question, "How many jobs did ye create?" This question indicates either a critic having his pound of flesh or an ignorance of the process of community enterprise.

Community enterprise rarely creates jobs. Private investment is usually the essential ingredient for job creation. Budgetary restrictions ensure that any jobs created via community enterprise are few in number. The suspicion is always that only "funny jobs" are created by community enterprise. This is often the reason for the still-birth of community initiatives or the avoidance of the essential task of endeavouring to increase the number of jobs available in a locality.

In reviewing the progress of the planning process of IRD Kiltimagh Limited, the facilitation, as distinct from the creation, of jobs is the first essential item to be placed under the microscope.

Job Facilitation: An Chéad Chéim

Jobs	Targets 1991–93	Results April 1994
Full-Time Jobs	30	69
Part-Time Jobs	67	52
FÁS Training Schemes	Nil	124

Note 1: The figures for job facilitation do not include jobs created by investors who received grant-assistance from the LEADER programme via the administrative offices of IRD Kiltimagh and who were external to the Kiltimagh Area (see LEADER programme Review).

Note 2: The jobs indicated above are those which were facilitated by way of the company's direct involvement in enticing investment into productive businesses in the area, or by direct investment by the company in business projects.

Population Trends

Official Statistics

Area	1981	1986	Change %	1991	Change %
Kiltimagh Town	1,145	982	–14.2	952	–3.1
Kiltimagh District Electoral Division	1,578	1,395	–11.6	1,309	–6.2

Returning Emigrants

No official statistics are available on emigration or its opposite — immigration. For the purposes of this review, a member of the board of directors of the company (who had returned to Kiltimagh from the UK since 1990) was requested to record the names and number of emigrants who, to his knowledge, had returned to the area over the previous three years. His head-count revealed more than 150 returning emigrants. To assess the number who had emigrated during the same period proved impossible, but undoubtedly the Kiltimagh Diaspora is not yet finished and much more remains to be done to stem the flow.

UCD Environmental Institute Assessment

In July 1992 (at the request of The Enterprise Trust), the Environmental Institute at University College Dublin produced a brief analysis of the business generation potential of local area development generated by IRD Kiltimagh. The following is a summary of the analysis:

Local Impacts

- Payroll generation: Gross £599,852; Net: £462,952
- Gross output generated: £1,588,550
- Employment generated: 125.

The employment estimated to have been generated by IRD Kiltimagh area is as follows:

Activity	Number Employed	Payroll Gross £	Payroll Net £
Industry	21	218,400	136,500
Services	22	176,000	121,000
FÁS Training	43	127,452	127,452
Full-Time	86	521,852	384,952
Part-Time	39	78,000	78,000
Total	125	599,852	462,952

Note: Assumptions re numbers employed and wages paid are set out in Annex A. It is estimated that 23 per cent of the wages bill [(1 — 462,952/599,852) x 100] is paid in taxes, etc., but this still leaves almost £0.46 million circulating in the economy. We make the (very strong) assumption that none of this activity would have happened without the IRD.

Local Expenditure Effects

We can apply the distribution of household income in the West, as estimated in the Household Budget Survey 1987, to the total net income of £462,952 to yield the following:

Item	%	£ *
Food	27.2	125,900
Drink & Tobacco	7.9	36,600
Clothing & Footwear	8.4	38,900
Fuel & Light	6.9	31,900
Housing	6.6	30,600
Non-Durable Household Goods	2.2	10,200
Durable Household Goods	4.0	18,500
Miscellaneous Goods	3.7	17,100
Transport	14.2	65,700
Services and Other	18.9	87,500
Total	100.0	462,900

* Rounded to the nearest £100.

Net Local Sectoral Impacts

Applying the Household Budget Survey coefficients for the West region to the Kiltimagh data, the following sectoral distribution emerges:

Item	%	£ *
Food	27.2	125,900
Services and Other	18.9	87,500
Transport	14.2	65,700
Clothing & Footwear	8.4	38,900
Drink & Tobacco	7.9	36,600
Fuel & Light	6.9	31,900
Housing	6.6	30,600
Durable Household Goods	4.0	18,500
Miscellaneous Goods	3.7	17,100
Non-Durable Household Goods	2.2	10,200
Total	100.0	462,900

* Rounded to the nearest £100.

These flows will boost economic activity commensurably in the sectors involved.

National Multipliers

The gross output of IR£1,588,550 will have a modest multiplier locally (probably 1.1 to 1.2) but, as it works its way through the national economy, it exceeds 1.6. (Source: Percentages from Central Statistics Office, 1989. Household Budget Survey 1987, Volume I (p. 200).)

Note: This overstates expenditure somewhat, as it assumes that there are no savings. How much will stay in the local economy is unknown, but much of the "first round" expenditure on food (£125,900); drink (£38,900); and housing (£30,600) will add cash-flow to local traders.

Implications for National Gross Output

If we assume that the ratio of wages to output nationally in wooden products, furniture, and lodging/catering services can be applied to industry and services respectively in Kiltimagh, we can apply the following coefficients to the wage estimates: Ratio of Total Output to Wages: 3.8 : 2.5 (See Annex A).

Activity	Wages £	Gross Output £
Industry	218,400	829,920
Services (including FÁS and Part-Time)	303,452	758,630
Total	521,852	1,588,550

It is unlikely that the activity generated in Kiltimagh would imply such increases in gross output, because these jobs are added at the margin, and do not represent "average" national performance. In Annex B can be seen the multipliers in terms of activity generated in other sectors as a result of a £1 expansion in final sales for the industrial and services sectors in question. We don't know how much of the gross output shown in Table for Local Sectoral Impacts (above) is added to final demand (households and exports) so we can't estimate how much of the sectoral multiplier to apply. It is interesting to note that the service sector makes a much bigger contribution to GDP than the industrial sector, because of the large "leakage" to export of the former.

Banking Activity

In preparation for the local shopping promotion campaign of 1990/91, the two banks in Kiltimagh — AIB and Bank of Ireland — were asked to supply details on banking activity in the area, based on one week's activity in February 1990 — a quiet period in business circles. Four years later, for the same week in February 1994, the results revealed a startling increase in activity.

Banking Activity	1990 £	1994 £	Change %
Lodgements of Commercial Enterprises			
Bank 1	200,000	313,000	+ 56.5
Bank 2	142,2311	272,860	+ 33
Lodgements of Retail Shops			
Bank 1	269,000	407,000	+ 51
Bank 2	47,721	46,430	− 3
Total Lodgements			
Bank 1	269,000	407,000	+ 51
Bank 2	189,952	319,290	+ 68
Totals for Kiltimagh	458,952	726,290	+ 58

Summary of Financial Statements

In keeping with good business practice, the accounts of the company were audited to 31 December each year, commencing in 1991. The results are compared here with the initial projected annual figures set out in the Company Prospectus in 1989.

	Projected 1989 £000	Actual 1990 £000	Actual 1991 £000	Actual 1992 £000	Actual 1993 £000
Annual Income	70	104	190	246	213
Annual Expenditure	70	48	85	224	208
Total Net Assets	Nil	51	205	296	298

Visitors and Observations

During the period 1990–94, it is estimated that 1,500 people visited Kiltimagh from Ireland and overseas each year as observers of the IRD Kiltimagh Programme. The casual observations of some visitors were recorded during the period.

"It's about a year since I was here and I drove up and down twice to digest the marvellous improvements which are so obvious."
Mr Padraic Flynn, TD, Minister for Justice, June 1991

"Where would Kiltimagh be now if you hadn't started?"
Mr Des Mahon, Mayo County Manager, 1992

"We have been inspired by the unbelievable success of the IRD Kiltimagh Group. The results in Kiltimagh have been startling."
Ms Marie Creighton, Ad Hoc Committee, IRD Claremorris, May 1992

"I haven't been in Kiltimagh for years and I couldn't believe that the place had improved so much."
Pat Monaghan, Sligo, at the Western Bishops' Conference, June 1992

"When you enter the town, you get the feeling of it being a lovely quaint town."
Colin Whittington, UK Business Consultant, July 1992

"I can't believe the big change in such a short time."
James Morrissey, Sunday Business Post

"Kiltimagh is leading the way in showing what can be achieved in a short period by dedicated hard work."
Mary O'Rourke, Minister for Trade and Tourism, 1992

"This is everything I always wanted to see in rural development."
Mark Killilea, Euro MEP, 1993

"My visit to Mayo has been made so much richer and satisfactory by this presentation of what you have achieved."
Mr Liam Hyland, Minister for Rural Development, 1993

On 22 February 1994, poet Robin Mellor visited Kiltimagh. A collection of poems, *Welsh Rhubarb*, is one of his many contributions to the development of the arts in the UK. Blizzard conditions prevailed during his visit to Kiltimagh. In a complimentary letter, he wrote:

I was very impressed by the efforts of the residents of Kiltimagh to make something special of their town and its culture. You all deserve as much support as possible. Please accept the enclosed poem as a token of my thanks for a very interesting visit to Kiltimagh.

Dawn, Co. Mayo, 22 February 1994
Chiaroscuro. Wind batters water.
Resolute grey. Some clouds mimce
the mountains. Flamingo sky
ribbles ribbed feathers. Reeds
genuflect a greeting. The day sneaks in.

Enter the sun, lifting itself from
a dark mountain bed, yawn
disfigured face. Sycophantic
clouds extend a welcome
edged with royal colour.

Later snow lay on the ground
for the first time in ten years.

Significant Expenditures in Kiltimagh Area by Development Agencies Working with IRD Kiltimagh Limited

Development agencies working with IRD Kiltimagh Limited incurred significant expenditures in support of the company's development plan. These expenditures are outlined below in recognition of the agencies' contributions.

FÁS, The Training and Employment Authority	£
Social Employment Schemes	128,467
Teamwork Schemes	25,748
Employment Subsidy Scheme	14,040
Training Programmes:	
Food Production	86,300
Craft Producers Course	73,000
Community Youth Training Programmes:	
Enterprise Centre	60,208
Kiltimagh Historical Society/Cill Aodáin Churchyard	105,975
Community Enterprise Programme:	
Project Manager	26,000
Total	519,738

Industrial Development Authority	£
Feasibility Study: Enterprise Centre	7,400
Feasibility Study: Food Production	12,500
Capital Assistance: Enterprise House	97,560
Management Consultancy	25,000
Total	142,460

Mayo County Development Team	£
Management Grant	30,000
Data Services Business	3,000
Training Centre	3,300
Total	36,300

Mayo County Council	£
Development of Enterprise House *	60,000

*   This does not include many additional infrastructural developments in the area that are associated with the Planning Process but which also could be regarded by the Council as core development work.

Ireland West Tourism	£
Development of Facilities	57,373
Marketing	10,000
Town Square Improvements	5,000
Total	72,373

Note: Assistance to Venture-Capital companies as associates of IRD Kiltimagh Limited is excluded from the above.

LEADER Programme

In 1992, IRD Kiltimagh Limited became an administrative office for Western Rural Development Limited. In two years, £835,162 was allocated to projects from the Kiltimagh Office.

The following general areas were involved in project development: Aughamore, Bohola, Charlestown, Kilkelly, Kiltimagh, Knock and Swinford. The total investment in the area from these projects was £2,100,000, and 60 full-time and 68 part-time jobs were created from this involvement.

15
Conversion of Weaknesses to Strengths

One main overall objective of community enterprise must be to convert, in part or in total, the recognised weaknesses of a region into strengths.

SWOT Analysis

In 1991, IRD Kiltimagh Limited, in its Company Business Plan — An Chéad Chéim — undertook a SWOT (Strengths, Weaknesses, Opportunities and Threats) Analysis. The following report identified the significant points:

Strengths

(i)   The proximity of Horan International Airport (15 km) and of Knock Shrine (8 km)

(ii)   The proximity of the River Moy (10 minutes drive) and its major tributaries

        Note: The town of Kiltimagh is located on high ground between the River Pollagh and the River Glore, which converge north of the town to form the River Gweestion, a major tributary of the Moy. The Moy is one of the best salmon rivers in Europe

(iii)   The proximity of Lough Conn and other under-utilised local lakes, and nine rivers which are excellent for trout and coarse fishing

(iv)   An unspoiled natural environment of hills, river valleys and bogland

(v)   The central location of the town within Mayo/Connaught, with all the large towns of the region — Galway, Athlone, Sligo, Castlebar, Westport and Ballina — less than an hour's drive away

(vi)   A young educated workforce from the local second-level schools, who have an excellent educational background, qualifications and skills

(vii)   A strong local sense of community and tradition with many local clubs and voluntary organisations

(viii)   Many archaeological, legendary and historical associations.

(ix)   The name of the town, Kiltimagh, and its association with the term, "Culchie", which is now included in the *Oxford English Dictionary* — the term meaning "ordinary rural folk".

Weaknesses

Note: Where "Weaknesses" have been partly converted to "Strengths", they are indicated by the symbol +.

(i)   Poor land quality with limited agricultural output as a result

(ii)   Small farm sizes with part-time farmers constituting a high proportion of those on the land

(iii)   +   Fact that Kiltimagh has gone through a period of economic stagnation and business decline

(iv)   +   The number of young people who emigrate, which leads to lack of re-investment in farms and businesses

(v)   +   The commercial strengths of adjacent towns — Castlebar, Ballina, and Claremorris, for example — which lead to a leakage of retail spending power from the town and lack of re-investment in businesses

(vi)   +   With no main route through the town, the absence of any significant trade from passing traffic

(vii)   +   Unemployment

(viii)   +   Undeveloped agri-related employment potential

(ix)   +   Underdeveloped tourism activities

(x)   +   Poor public-transport facilities

(xi)   +   Litter and untidiness

(xii)   +   Unplanned painting, decorating, signwriting

(xiii)   +   Poor public/private landscaping

(xiv)   +   Lack of internal/external signposting

(xv)   +   Lack of cohesion between interest groups

(xvi)   +   The absence of a spirit of enterprise

(xvii)   +   The prevalence of a wage-packet and/or "hand-out" mentality.

External Opportunities

(i)   General improvement in key national economic indicators

(ii)   Lower inflation rates and lower prices

(iii)   Increased awareness in government and state agencies of the potential of tourism

(iv)   Greater international awareness of environmental conservation and unspoiled areas

(v)   Increased emphasis on demand for activity-related holidays and leisure time

(vi)   Growing demand for international summer schools in Irish cultural studies, in activity-related programmes and in English language studies for younger and adult students

(vii)   Emphasis on computer technology as scope for industrial development

(viii)   Increased awareness of the need for alternative farming programmes

(ix)   Increased awareness, both nationally and in the EU, of the need for rural development programmes.

External Threats

(i)   Probably the worst economic recession that the western world has experienced

(ii)   Direct national and international competition for activity-based holidays

(iii)   High cost of living

(iv)   Currency fluctuations

(v)   Reputation for poor hygiene standards

(vi)   Poor public transport

(vii)   Travel distance

(viii)   Pricing policies of airline/sea-ferry companies

(ix)   Trade disputes

(x)   The economic difficulties being experienced by those in the traditional mainstream farming activities.

16

Facilitation Review

The members of the board of directors were facilitated over a period in order to ascertain their views on the progress of the company. The facilitation and subsequent lengthy report (here abbreviated) was undertaken by Mary Keane, Director, Greenfield Co-ordinators.

Review and Planning Programme 1993–94, IRD Kiltimagh Limited

Introduction

The local representatives of the board of IRD Kiltimagh Limited have come together over a series of five meetings to review the company's business plans for 1990–93 and to make submissions for the planning period 1994–99. This process is intended as a type of thermometer by which to assess the health of the company to date and to prescribe for its future well-being. The control and planning process is effectively the realistic managerial responsibility of the local community representatives. It is a task which must be undertaken with energy and commitment if the community company is to operate as a dynamic and efficient entity. It is anticipated that, at the conclusion of this programme, community representatives will have:

- Reviewed the current position of the company and the community.
- Established a "vision" (mission statement) for the future.
- Indicated the appropriate strategies for identified objectives.
- Ear-marked the necessary resources in human and financial terms.
- Examined the future role of the local management team.
- Prepared strategies for further local involvement at managerial level.

The following programme objectives have been set in place:

- Programme Objective (i) Review: To review IRD Kiltimagh Limited at the end of its current three-year planning period under the headings: (a) Changes, (b) Problems, (c) Major Successes/Achievements
- Programme Objective (ii) Vision: To establish what vision the local community representatives have for IRD Kiltimagh Limited for the next five years

- Programme Objective (iii) Company Objectives: To focus and state precisely the company objectives for the 1994–99 planning period
- Programme Objective (iv) Strategies: To establish the appropriate strategies to be undertaken so as to achieve the above stated objectives
- Programme Objective (v) Resources: To draw up a list of resources that will be needed for the planning period 1994–99, to include human, property and financial resources
- Programme Objective (vi) The Team: To determine how best the local community representatives can contribute and work as a good dynamic team.

Report on Findings and Discussion

Objective 1 — Review
Changes:

(i)   Improved town appearance in general

(ii)   Improvement in people's attitudes

(iii)   New tourism-related facilities

(iv)   Traffic jams in Aiden Street — considered as a positive change but also negative

(v)   Potential top-class hotel facility in town

(vi)   Considerable improvement in shopping and availability of goods and services

(vii)   Smaller groups of begrudgers

(viii) No change in some derelict sites

(ix)   Crystal Ballroom still remaining in its former state

(x)   Increase in town population of 150+ people since plan commenced

(xi)   Improved employment.

Problems:

(i)   People are afraid to make decisions at board level.

(ii)   Front-of-house management of IRD good. However, office operational structure needs to be more clearly defined and become more efficient.

(iii)   There exists a "blur" between voluntary community sector and management, because of inadequate communication.

(iv)   IRD Kiltimagh Limited has highs and lows. There is a need for consistency in progressing projects which are undertaken.

(v)   There is a lack of information and inadequate time is given to voluntary sector prior to making important board decisions.

(vi)   There is too much IRD involvement in the ownership of start-up businesses in the Enterprise Centre.

(vii)   IRD is failing to provide guidance and support for the over-50s and the young.

(viii)   Promotion to community has not been as it should be: could be improved.

Major Achievements and Successes:

(i)   Kiltimagh has national and international recognition in rural development domain.

(ii)   There have been overall improvements in all aspects of community life.

(iii)   IRD Kiltimagh Limited has proved that the process can work and that its approach is proving to be the best relative approach.

17
Planning Ahead

In planning for the period 1995–99, the company took the unusual step in community enterprise of treating 1994 as a Review Year. The first period of the year was spent on analysis, the second period on planning for the future. Analysis and planning, however, are not mutually exclusive, and hence ran concurrently.

The process involved the following:

(i)   A series of five meetings, using a professional facilitator, with representatives of the local community on the board of directors. In the latter stages, each invited a companion to attend the review process in order to generate a greater interest in community development.

(ii)   A general public meeting on development.

(iii) Meetings to discuss social issues and the formulation of support groups where necessary.

(iv)   A study of the Community Development Programme under the auspices of the Department of Social Welfare. This was undertaken with the assistance of the Department and involved visits to groups in Waterford, Dublin, Cork and Donegal.

(v)   An invitation to external non-community directors of the board to provide observations.

(vi)   Meetings with ongoing working groups to advance community projects.

(vii) Brainstorming on new projects which needed to be undertaken and the allocation of working-group leaders to these projects.

(viii) Workshops involving professional management in the preparation of a framework entitled, "Kiltimagh — The

Artisan Village" and in allocating projects within this framework.

(ix)   A FÁS Community Enterprise Programme (Module A) with a select group from the community.

(x)   A Schools Educational Programme: IRD staff visited local primary and second-level schools, with the purpose of telling the story of IRD and also highlighting its future aspirations.

The following plans for the period 1995–99 evolved from the above procedure.

Three main objectives will be developed as follows:

(1)   To implement a programme for the development of the living aspects of the adopted theme. This involves small business and traditional craft development programmes.

(2)   To implement a programme of interpretation of the in-digenous historical aspects of the adopted theme.

(3)   To develop complementary activities that respond to the demands of those who wish to experience the afore-mentioned development, and to the demands of the local population and visitors to the general area, including visitors to Knock Marian Shrine.

Plans for the Period 1995–99

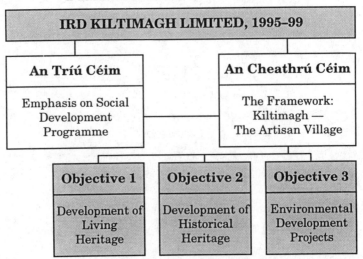

Implementing the Artisan Theme

Objective

To implement a programme for the development of the living aspects of the adopted theme. This involves small business and traditional craft development programmes.

Background

A number of aspects have been assisted/developed such as:

- The provision of workspace for small businesses
- A stained-glass studio — Kiltimagh Stained Glass
- Hand-crafted jewellery — Kilticraft
- Millinery
- Increasing numbers of suppliers to The Farmhouse Pantry
- Courses in traditional crafts
- Courses in fresh-food production
- The development of the Artists' Retreat Park
- The proposed development of a Conservatoire of Music for the North-West Region.

Strategy for Development

(i)   Launch a development programme to attract three different types of activity to the village and its environs:

◊   Home/farm-fresh food producers

◊   Hand-crafts producers

◊   Aesthetic artists.

(ii)   Conduct a resource audit of competent artisans in the locality.

(iii)   Provide workspace at appropriate locations.

(iv)   Continue to develop the brand image of "The Farmhouse Pantry" as a marketing tool for fresh-food producers.

(v)   Provide office and other facilities for Mayo Community Arts Network and encourage the development of Meitheal Kiltimagh Arts Network.

(vi)   Provide a financial and advisory assistance package for developing artisans.

(vii) Prepare an assistance package for small shopkeepers to preserve the authenticity of their business in keeping with the theme.

(viii) Support the CUT campaign which creates public awareness of supporting small businesses in Ireland.

(ix)   Provide a comprehensive networking system for all three categories at (i) above.

(x)   Liaise with cross-border institutions involved in the teaching of a better quality of music and seek to have a third-level qualification applied to this activity.

Implementing an Interpretative Programme

Objective

To implement a programme of interpretation of the indigenous historical aspects of the adopted theme.

Background

As part of "An Chéad Chéim" programme 1991–93, IRD Kiltimagh Limited outlined the following goals:

(i)   That the Kiltimagh townscape will gradually over the next four years begin to reflect the theme "A nineteenth-century market town"

(ii)   That the theme will distinguish Kiltimagh from other Irish towns

(iii) That this will be a "cause célèbre" for the inhabitants

(iv)   That this distinctiveness will be a source of attraction to outsiders.

In 1992 "An Dara Céim" was launched with the following development goals:

(i)   Community Arts Programme

(ii)   Sculpture Symposium

(iii) Theatre and Artists' Retreat

(iv)   Cultural/Artistic Centre.

Work has already been started on the completion of the Kiltimagh Heritage Trail, including the Cill Aodáin monastic site, the Ballinamore church site, Cultrasna village, the Railway Station and Mooney's Ring Fort.

Strategy for Development

(i)   Seek tenders from consultants to the tourism sector to provide appropriate documentation on the history and modern-day facilities in Kiltimagh that are relevant to the theme.

(ii)   Form an Interpretative Committee for the theme, The Artisan Village. This will be achieved by networking with existing bodies like Kiltimagh Historical Society.

(iii)   Await the publication of *The History of Kiltimagh*, which is being researched by a former native, Mr Peter Sobolewski.

(iv)   Have famous natives and associates appropriately commemorated in sculpture or in other art forms.

(v)   Prepare an audit of sites of historical and local interest.

(vi)   Where appropriate have these highlighted and/or access provided, bearing in mind the need to conserve the authenticity of these.

(vii)   Provide documentation, signposting and guides to these sites.

(viii) Continue with incentives to local businesses to preserve or alter business frontages to complement the theme.

(ix)   Complete the development of Kiltimagh Heritage Trail.

(x)   Complete Cultrasna Penal Village development.

Developing Complementary Activities

Objective

To develop complementary activities that respond to the demands of those who wish to experience the aforementioned development and to the demands of the local population and visitors to the general area, including visitors to Knock Marian Shrine.

Background

Kiltimagh has already developed various aspects of a comprehensive rural tourism programme.

Accommodation in the area includes 66 ITB-approved beds in Bed and Breakfast houses. The beautifully presented Cill Aodáin Hotel (Two Star) has all modern facilities and 40 additional beds.

Facilities available locally include:

- The Town Hall Theatre and Artists' Retreat Centre
- The Station Master's House Exhibition Centre
- The Town Museum
- The Sculpture Park
- The Venture Fun Park
- The Town Forge Museum
- Cill Aodáin Monastic Site
- Mooney's Ring Fort
- Initial work at Cultrasna Penal Village.

Development on the townscape includes:

- Traditional shop-fronts
- Underground cable network
- Traditional street-lighting
- Soft landscaping
- Stone-wall repair and replacement.

Kiltimagh needs to attract investment for further tourism amenities that will provide the critical mass necessary for its development as a Rural Tourism Centre. The aim is to attract and aid the development of projects complementary to the required critical mass of tourism attractions for the village and its environs in order to become a complete centre of rural tourism.

Strategy for Development

The amenities to be developed include:

(i)   A Conservatoire of Music — In developing its projects, the development company has always indicated its wish to get involved in one large project. The completion of workspace facilities was first undertaken. In its next phase of planning, a detailed submission has been prepared for a Conservatoire of Music. The aim is to purchase suitable premises and to convert it into a Conservatoire of Music for the North-West Region, incorporating teaching and recording facilities with a good-quality residential provision.

(ii)   The provision of display and retention facilities for artistic groups who build floats for town festivals and other parades.

(iii) The development of a children's "Fun Factory" to provide indoor facilities for children to complement the outdoor Venture Park.

(iv)   The provision of an outdoor go-karting facility. Go-karting is proving extremely popular. This facility could be provided by private investment as an extra attraction for the town.

(v)   The provision of additional accommodation bases to provide extra facilities to be incorporated with the existing Cill Aodáin Hotel and the 66 approved Bed and Breakfast spaces in the town. This to include: a hostel with emphasis on outdoor-pursuit seekers and in particular for walking activists; caravan and camping park with indoor gym facilities, including table tennis, badminton and other games in Kiltimagh Community School.

(vi)   To provide a ten-pin bowling facility at a suitable location.

(vii) An Indoor Activity Centre for adults and children. This to include: swimming pool (size to be determined); sauna room; steam room; Jacuzzi bath; gymnasium and health studio, to be developed by private investment.

Finances

The following tables give some indication of the financial needs and ambitions of IRD Kiltimagh Limited in the period 1995–99.

Projected Capital Investment Programme, 1995–99

Category	Amount £000	Community £000	Local Venture Capital £000	Public Funds £000	External Venture Capital £000	Sundry £000
Village Enhancement	322	16.0	80.0	218	—	8
Community Arts Programme	120	12.0	15.0	60	10.0	23
Tourism Infrastructure	800	40.0	200.0	360	180.0	20
Industrial Workspace Development	400	20.0	80.0	180	110.0	10
Seed Capital Programme	180	9.0	45.0	81	—	45
Family Farm Programme	340	17.0	85.0	153	30.0	55
Tourism Marketing Programme	120	6.0	20.0	60	20.0	14
Telecottages Services Programme	150	7.5	37.5	75	20.0	10
Training Development	154	2.7	2.0	127	2.3	20
Housing Development	250	60.0	—	188	—	2
Employment Schemes	184	4.0	20.0	130	20.0	10
	3,020	194.2	584.5	1,632	392.3	217

Projected Annual Operating Costs, 1995–99

Operating Budget: *Annual Operating Costs*	*£000*
General Management, Secretarial and Office Administration	65
Business Development Management	18
Community Development Management	18
Tourism Development	15
Agricultural Development	22
LEADER Project Management	27
Training and Community Capacity Building	18
Community Arts Development	17
	200

Operating Budget: Projected Sources of Finance	*£000*
Local Community Subscription	25
Business Income Generation	28
FÁS Training and Employment	30
Mayo County Enterprise Board	25
IDA	12
LEADER Programme Administration	35
Enterprise Trust	25
Farming Co-operative Sponsorship	15
Other Sponsorship	5
	200

Section 3:
A Philosophy of Community Enterprise

18
Community Enterprise

Why plan for community enterprise? Many, if not most, community development organisations have existed and successfully developed their activities without any pre-prepared plan. Nonetheless, the movement advocating strategic planning for community enterprise continues to grow. As one who fully supports this movement, I believe that it is time we looked more carefully at the need for strategic planning if community enterprise is to advance and if it is to have the courage to facilitate real and significant job opportunities. That the creation of real jobs can be stimulated and facilitated has been proven in Kiltimagh.

Community enterprise is the energy which:

- Comes from human resources combining to create a force for action in a community
- Endeavours to stimulate projects for the benefit of the entire community, directly or indirectly, and economically, socially or culturally, and
- Will be a reason for the advancement of the "pride-of-place" being developed within the community.

The "community" can be taken to mean either people resident in a specific geographical area or a community of interest. In the latter case, a group of individuals who come together to promote a specific sectoral programme for their own benefit can be defined as a community of interest. Generally, however, and for the purpose of this book, I have confined my focus to community enterprise in specific geographical areas.

Principles of Community Enterprise

From my experiences of service to community enterprise, both as a voluntary worker and as a professional manager, I suggest the following principles for the proper functioning of community enterprise.

I choose the term "community enterprise" because of my reservations about the connotations of the word "development", and because I contend that what is commonly known as community development is enterprising in all facets both economic and social. Enterprise is variously defined as "an important, difficult or dangerous plan to be tried".

A community enterprise organisation must:

- Be primarily concerned with the advancement of the community
- Be accessible to all sectors of the community
- Act in the best interests of the geographical area it seeks to serve
- Be conducted with openness and transparency and with justice and fairness, to encourage confidence and participation
- Be willing to serve and facilitate rather than to impose
- Be the champion of the marginalised sectors
- Be willing to forge links with the outside world for the betterment of all
- Foster a climate of support to allow locals and outsiders to be of further service to the community
- Offer a vision for the ongoing development of community resources to create a focus for pre-defined planning for specific action periods which will be adhered to.

The Steps of Community Enterprise

The three main steps of community enterprise are:

- The Creation of Awareness
- Planning
- Action.

The Creation of Awareness

There is considerable difficulty in creating awareness of the needs of communities. This step is often described as the "Pre-

Development Phase". Very often these needs are not recognised by locals, and the first steps towards awareness creation come from an outsider who comes to reside in the area. The objectivity of the newcomer can be the trigger that begins the process. Unfortunately, too often, the outsider can overdo the criticism and be dismissed as a "blow-in". Sensitively handled, however, the objectivity of the newcomer, combined with local leadership, can kindle the flame of awareness.

The pre-development phase must be carefully handled and, once again, the use of professionals is advocated. A key requirement is that all agendas, including hidden agendas of vested interests, be put on the table. There is a need to emphasise at this point that there is nothing wrong with being involved in the development process for selfish reasons such as the development of one's own business. The recognition and development of a symbiotic relationship is vital for the success of community enterprise.

The creation of awareness also requires the use of field-trips to study what others are doing. This is typified by the number of people who come to Kiltimagh to see the development process in action.

Planning

The use of planning is emphasised throughout the Kiltimagh story. There are several aspects to planning that need emphasis:

- The preparation of the plan must involve the local community. Taking soundings is essential. When soundings are completed, however, someone must do the writing. This is where the involvement of a creative professional is essential.

- The plan must reflect teamwork through small working groups.

- The plan must be specific, yet achievable. It should be written in simple language with a minimum of analysis and with a maximum of suggested actions and strategies.

- The plan should be costed in its entirety, including community inputs by way of sponsorship or "sweat equity".

- Attention to the training needs associated with the proposed developments is essential. There is a need to build the capacity of the community to continue the organic development process.

Action

This is the most essential ingredient of community enterprise. The world is full of reports on the need for action. Paralysis by analysis is a particular curse in Ireland. The need to act is paramount.

The actions to be undertaken must provide autonomy for working groups to implement their plans. This autonomy should not be confused with isolation. There is a need for a facilitative support structure for the working groups. Personal development through community development is also vital as a reward for voluntary effort.

The action plan must be time-limited. The need to indicate a starting time and a finishing time is vital. In the past, many well-intentioned community workers have been turned off by the failure to set deadlines. With no exit mechanism other than total abandonment of what they feel is obviously a worthwhile project, they come to see it as a millstone around their necks and are reluctant to get involved in further projects. This is detrimental to both the development process and the community in general.

The action to be taken must also include reviewing progress on a regular basis and setting a time for a complete review of the project.

19
Getting Started

There is little known about communities at crisis point, except that when a community recognises that it has arrived thereat, the stimulation to act to prevent final demise is very strong. But what or where or when is crisis point? Perhaps I can explain in an anecdote.

During my time as Manager, I was visited by a community group from a town near Kiltimagh. The members were enthralled as we told our story using "before" and "after" slides to illustrate the change in the area. Inevitably, the discussion came to focus on what their own area might do and how it might get started. And then came the comment:

> "Ah sure, it was easy to see how Kiltimagh needed it, but it's different in our town. D'ya see, we have good factories and shops whereas Kiltimagh was dead."

This story is recounted regularly for visiting groups. Despite warnings about the dangers of complacency, the mind-set was wrong and, needless to say, the process has, as of yet, not even begun in that town.

Another town not far from Galway City was later to be the subject of discussion for advice, and again the lack of a sense of crisis became the central topic. On this occasion, I insisted that we spend a few minutes defining what crisis meant for that area. Then it began to dawn.

> "Yes, the identity of our area is being subsumed into the larger urban centre. Our children no longer have a clear identity with their own community."

It was agreed also that economic leakage was rife. Businesses were closing or being sucked into the larger centre. Community effort was dormant as a result of all this.

The crisis point is different for each area and the need for community protection is no different from the protection process of any commercial business. In other words, community development can only be advancing or retarding. It will only stand still for very brief periods, if at all.

Getting People Together

To start the process of community enterprise, the first essential is to get people together. This should be done by public invitations — in writing, on community noticeboards, to be read at community gatherings, or in churches. Any community organiser will tell you that you can count on a one-third attendance from written invitations sent to those thought to be committed. So be prepared and don't be disappointed. It's not you, it's the system.

The late Fr James McDyer of Glencolumcille confirmed, as regards community development:

> "One-third are sympathetic, one-third are apathetic and one-third don't give a damn."

Therefore, make sure that you also make personal contact with the people whom you need to have in attendance, while at the same time having performed the necessary function of public invitation.

It is also worth remembering the adage about quality of attendance versus quantity of attendance. The only time you need quantity is on publicity-seeking occasions. Other than at such times, you can be sure that the smaller the group of committed individuals, the more likely it is that the work will be done.

Remember also that the person or persons who start this process of getting people together may not eventually be the best person(s) to lead the community to "the promised land". The skills required for leadership may be different from the skills required for attracting the first audience to a preliminary meeting.

The Planning Chart

The first requirement for community enterprise planning is to agree on:

- The planning period (a start date and a finish date)
- When to begin the next planning period.

I visualise enterprise planning as a series of rhombi:

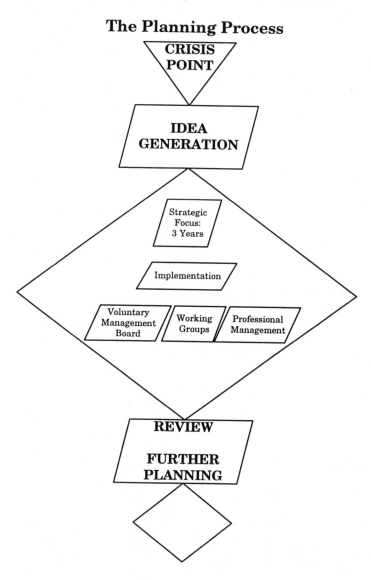

The Planning Process

A community will normally have experienced a crisis point before initiating the planning process. The top apex of each rhombus is the starting point for implementation. The centre is the total span of the plan being implemented — within the boundaries and always in focus. Activity will eventually lessen or narrow as the plan nears completion. The bottom apex is the point of review. This apex is conveniently linked with the next rhombus, indicating the obvious link between the review period of previous plans and the starting point of the next phase of planning.

Frequently the rhombi may overlap, as one set of plans becomes superimposed on a previous set indicating an increase in community stimulation and activity — further evidence of the dynamic of successful strategic planning.

The diagram shows that the strategic planning process provides a specific focus within an overall vision, indicating where we see our community heading over the next three or four years. From the point of view of professional management, the plan provides the manager with an agreed direction within which to operate. The competent and self-assured manager will focus on this plan and will refuse to be subjected to reactive demands.

Planning will also satisfy investors in projects and will reassure sponsors and patrons. It will prove to subscribers that their money is being used with a sense of purpose and direction. In the current competitive climate, it is now essential to have an overall plan to produce when applying for state assistance. This helps state agency personnel to see specific projects in a global context rather than in isolation.

The need for monitoring and control is no less essential in community enterprise than in business, to ensure both responsible decision-making and accountability. Hence a review module should be indicated at the end of each planning period.

At this point, and to illustrate the distinction, note that a community enterprise plan should never be conical or open-ended in shape. This has been the case in far too many communities in the past where no review period was defined, no timescales were set even though there were obvious milestones along the way.

A Community Plan is Not ...

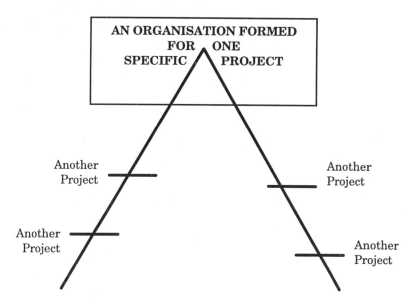

AN ORGANISATION FORMED
FOR ONE
SPECIFIC PROJECT

Another Project

Another Project

Another Project

Another Project

Be Prepared

Every public gathering has its share of difficult people. I have rarely worked with a community where the "It won't work" individual hasn't been present. So be prepared, allow them enough of a say but don't allow them to dominate. This is where a good chairperson is essential.

Despite a plea to local political activists to allow community enterprise to progress without "playing politics", you can be sure that flag-wavers of different types, including those with political flags will be present. These people usually wear a number of different hats. Have patience, however, and they may learn how to wear one hat at a time with appropriate elegance. Again the chair must be prepared to expose their game gently.

There is also a breed who regards it as a duty to take positions on every committee and who never participates other than to watch their corner in order to keep their particular flag flying.

Then let us not forget "the old guard", the people who don't want things to change because it will expose their failures in the past. "Around here, we always did it this way" is a certain tune. This group will disappear into the woodwork as you make a success of your plan.

20
The Elements of Community Enterprise

I have already referred to the three most important aspects of enterprising communities as:

(i)   Built Environment Renewal (BER)

(ii)   Local Economic Innovation (LEI)

(iii)   Social and Cultural Stimulation (SCS).

The ideal community plan has aspects of all three elements contained within it. With limited resources of money, with demands on state assistance from all sides, and with limited human resources in our voluntary sector, we can only strive to ensure that as much as possible of each element is contained in our planning.

Built Environment Renewal

BER is an absolutely essential aspect of community enterprise. For too long, however, community enterprise has been associated only with the renewal of the physical environment of a locality, because of the misconception that this was the total of community enterprise.

In a recent discussion with officials of the Department of Social Welfare, it was indicated to me that many aspects of the rural Community Development Programmes (which are supported by the Department and are supposed to be laden with emphasis on social development) invariably gallop towards the safe haven of built environmental renewal. Tackling the social development issues (which I refer to later) is difficult and very often "the old guard" refuses to get involved.

The easier option is to build the community centre, or to re-
new the market square, or to erect traditional lights, or to
build stone walls around graveyards or to improve the access
to villages. All of these activities are laudable in themselves,
but they should be seen for what they are — a sub-section of
community enterprise that is largely inorganic and finite in its
effects. Nevertheless, for the sake of public perception and of
seeing progress in action, the building of the community centre
or the replacement of stone walls are concrete (with apologies
for the pun) evidence that the system is working and that
"community development" is alive and well in a locality. Unfortunately, in today's world, perception is more important than
reality.

The reality is that these one-off projects are merely proof
that some group in the community has performed a worthwhile exercise in providing an additional facility. They suc-
ceeded in lobbying their local politician, they got their grant,
and hey presto! The tapes were cut, the grants were paid, votes
were guaranteed — and then nothing!

How often have we seen community centres, and other facilities, with no organised community spirit to ensure that the
facility is utilised? In some cases, we have even seen large
community centres built in a locality that is being decimated
by emigration or depopulation.

Does this mean that we should avoid the development aspects of built environmental renewal? On the contrary, as the
Kiltimagh story indicates, I believe that BER is an absolute
necessity if community enterprise is to succeed. All communities should be asked to provide a list of what is needed for BER
in their area. Where realistically compiled, the Built Environment Renewal list will be found to be finite — much to the
surprise of most. Unlike the other aspects of community enterprise, the full BER requirements for an area, which would
make that area a viable economic entity for the next 10 to 12
years, *can* be listed. The second phase of planning (second
rhombus) must, however, contain plans and schemes to ensure
that the facilities already provided will be used by good community organisations.

Imagine if our government had the courage to allow a Rural
Renewal Tax Incentive Scheme for a number of pilot areas

such as Killeshandra or Kiltimagh. No taxes would be lost because investment is negligible in these areas as they now stand. Why must it be just the inner-city or urban town renewals? Why discriminate? Why pull the investment money that is lying dormant in financial institutions of small towns into larger population centres in order to avail of the tax avoidance mechanisms of Urban Renewal Schemes.

Local Economic Innovation

In recent times, the emphasis on community participation in local economic enterprise has led to the building of Community Enterprise Centres (CECs) to replace the failed policy of building greenfield enterprise centres, many of which lie unoccupied at the edges of "carefully-selected" towns. In these cases, the bricks and mortar, or perhaps a political influence, predominated, and the necessary constant stimulation and "hand-holding" was left to chance.

This is the essential difference in the revised IDA (now Forbairt) programme — these centres now provide centralised administration systems. The integration of such administration systems into the new CEC programme has led to greater back-up for product development and innovation and thus to a more successful programme.

Where administration systems have been provided, very often with Forbairt support, workspace has been occupied and such centres are generally thriving and developing further.

The strategic development of this programme is essential. While all areas are now talking about enterprise centres, Forbairt must ensure that these centres do not lead perversely to job displacement, or quash the innovative aspects of the programme. Instead, a phased programme of strategic placement needs to be put in place.

The recent EU Community Initiative LEADER has provided an additional local impetus to project innovation through greater hands-on involvement at local level in developing projects. The lesson gradually being learned is that provision of workspace or grants is insufficient if ongoing permanent assistance at community level is unavailable. The days of a grant-dispensing agency being solely that will shortly disappear.

The lesson must be that giving the boatman a one-off grant to purchase a boat, and thereby a push into the middle of "Lake Start-up" without supplying him with a rudder, compass and constant navigational assistance, is of no long-term use. The graveyard of enterprise is littered with the wreckage of such boatmen.

A more pro-active approach to stimulating enterprise must be introduced throughout the state agencies. The type of hands-on assistance required lies not simply in training and retraining, although both of these are constant anchors. Advice on product development, quality control, business manage-ment, marketing, book-keeping and finance must all be avail-able and accessible locally.

This does not imply a host of increased overheads. Edu-cated, multi-skilled, business-oriented personnel can reduce the number of advisors to minuscule levels, while providing a direct interface with the local entrepreneur. I describe the local working of such a model in a later reference to televillages.

Similarly, the good-will of voluntary-sector involvement in community enterprise must also be availed of. Many local business-people are only too willing to become involved finan-cially in this aspect of community enterprise. Indeed, they may also wish to get involved in what they perceive as their strength of contribution, namely to be available as an advisory "think-tank" to discuss the problems of fledgling projects with business developers. The challenge is to ensure that this good-will opportunity is not lost and that invitations to participate are issued.

Social and Cultural Stimulation

Having discussed the physical environment and economic in-novation, I now introduce my views on the most important as-pect of community enterprise — Social and Cultural Stimula-tion. When I say the most important aspect, this does not mean that it should come first on the agenda. In fact, strategic planning for community enterprise may dictate otherwise.

The spirit and well-being of the human resources in our community are all important. How much spirit does a com-munity have? Is community activity indolent, passive, apa-thetic, indifferent or non-existent. If so, why, and what can be done about it? Are the marginalised to be given any part to play in community enterprise?

The number of trained personnel in our community who are capable of developing projects is also a vital factor. The standard of education is another. The general health and well-being of the community is another. The standard of living is another. The level of communications is yet another. And so we can go on, ad infinitum. Unlike BER, which can be capped within realistic limits by the circumstances of the environment, and LEI which is capped by want of innovation (and both of which are capped by want of monetary resources), Social and Cultural Stimulation is boundless. It is for this very reason that planning for its implementation is vital.

An in-depth study of the social needs of the local population needs to be undertaken. The results need to be analysed and, within the boundaries of the "likely", specific projects should be undertaken. There is a plethora of social needs in our communities. Some are very well catered for under existing systems. The Society of the St Vincent de Paul helps to keep body and soul together. "Meals on Wheels" does the same. Statutory agencies charged with health care undertake a myriad of tasks. Accordingly, there is no need to re-invent the wheel in the search for something worthwhile to do.

Our vision then may relate to other aspects of social need. The isolation of our elderly rural population is very often forgotten. The unemployed too need our support. The elderly in town and country may need a further stimulus or support group. Women's groups can provide great support for our female population. Lone parents' groups do excellent work for a growing sector of our society. Carers for the elderly are themselves too often uncared for. The list is endless. The fact that the list is endless is no reason to avoid the issue. On the contrary, because the list is endless there is all the more reason to plan a precise programme to answer these social needs.

A huge re-think needs to occur within our educational system and in our state training programmes. More specific job-related training needs to be available. Retraining programmes within work situations need greater emphasis. We hear boasts of our educational system — "a young well-educated population". But educated for what? Educated to look for the "job" instead of for "work"? Educated to believe that "Ireland owes me a living"? Educated to wait for the brown envelope as a farmer or an employee rather than for the incentive to get involved in a difficult but exciting new business idea?

Local enterprise planning must tackle these problems and needs. The state must provide the resources for more specific and local training and retraining. The state must take the lead in changing attitudes inculcated by our educational system. The creativity of the Irish in the cultural dimension has been acknowledged internationally. This has led to a sense of complacency and to the myth that cultural stimulation is rampant. Our system of propaganda on the success of the handful perpetuates this myth. While relishing the successes of the few who rose to fame, we forget to ask how much creative stimulation occurs in our own local community.

Perhaps you are one of the lucky ones. In my opinion, there is an abject failure within our centralised system of government to stimulate, to assist, or to recognise the massive latent talent that lies dormant at local level. The failure to assist local cultural and social stimulation, except in a hotchpotch manner, is hindering the unleashing of a massive vibrancy that exists in the "hidden Ireland".

Support for aspects of local cultural and artistic endeavour and for community arts programmes must be increased substantially. In the meantime, communities that fail to include some degree of social and cultural stimulation are also missing out on a huge area of potential economic and social enterprise. Community economic development will spring from increased community spirit, increased training and increased cultural activity.

The greatest regret I have regarding the first four years of IRD Kiltimagh's programme for development was the lack of such stimulation at various levels of community need. While community arts were included during the first four years, I have often expressed a view that we were not getting to the "hidden" Kiltimagh. Efforts to redress this imbalance were the reason for planning the programme, "An Tríú Céim".

21
The Strategic Community Enterprise Plan:
An Tríú Céim
(The Third Step)
(1995–99)

In planning for An Tríú Céim, the team listed the main problems and social needs of the Kiltimagh area. Many other communities will identify with these, and many will probably add to a list which could be endless. Our report is reproduced below.

The Main Problems

The region is characterised by a diversity of constraints and problems which are social, economic or physical in nature. The predominantly rural character of the area and its associated problems constitute a disadvantage both for the development of modern agriculture and for the establishment of new economic activities. The social development of the region is similarly constrained by a high degree of isolation and little or no public transport system.

The main problems that impede the economic and social development in the area are:

(i)   Low Income: The average GDP per capita of the region is about 75 per cent of the EU average. This restricts savings and investment and narrows the scope for initiative, enterprise and development.

(ii)   High Unemployment: Unemployment in the region is estimated at 20 per cent and remaining fairly stable with few apparent opportunities to absorb the rise in the numbers entering the labour force.

(iii)   High Emigration and Depopulation: The region is one of historically high emigration. It was one of the few to suffer a population decline during the period 1981–86 and this has accelerated in the meantime. The strong "pull" forces of emigration continue to predominate.

(iv)   Low Population Density: With a population that averages 10 per square kilometre, the density is less than half the national average. This increases infrastructural costs and impedes social cohesion.

(v)   Difficult Natural Conditions: The region has a high proportion of infertile, unproductive and difficult terrain and unfavourable climatic conditions, characterised by high rainfall and wind exposure.

(vi)   Low Productivity and Underemployment in Agriculture: The output per person is low at 75 per cent of the national average and there is a marked degree of underemployment. The area has few possible alternatives to conventional farming enterprise, because of physical and climatic constraints.

(vii)   Low Investment: Investment is constrained by imperfections in financial markets, infrastructural problems, poor information systems, occupational immobility, and inadequate appraisal of the area's potential.

(viii)   Isolation: A high degree of social isolation is prevalent. While many enjoy a nice rural life style, there are many others in the "hidden" Kiltimagh who suffer from social isolation.

Identified Needs

In reviewing the current state of community enterprise, the following needs are apparent:

(i)   A Resource Centre: As an open, warm and friendly service for meetings, casual calls, information dispensing, and as a refuge for those who need further care or support.

(ii)   Social Interaction and Support: The incredible level of isolation experienced by the disadvantaged elderly, by women in the home, by carers for disadvantaged relatives, by lone parents and by the unemployed is glaringly obvious. To a lesser degree, the handicapped need to be cared for in conjunction with the excellent support systems provided by Western Care Association, Rehab, and the Western Health Board in the local O'Hara Home.

(iii)   Citizen Information: The need to have their rights and entitlements explained more fully and more regularly to the young and to the disadvantaged is apparent. The large number of those who have to visit the monthly clinics of local public representatives to find such information needs to be facilitated in a more politically neutral environment.

(iv)   Facilitation of Community Enterprise: Those who have all the ingredients and spirit for involvement in community enterprise, in order to make a contribution to the betterment of all, need to feel that there is a place and that there are people who will listen calmly and patiently and who want them to become involved.

(v)   Advice on Business Development: A permanent need exists for a system of advice to be available to people who wish to start-up new businesses and to those already in business who find it difficult to purchase such advice but who need help to sustain their existing employment levels. This advice is needed not only by the disadvantaged but also by those who are endeavouring to provide a framework of employment in developing or protecting their businesses.

(vi)   Personal Development: A need exists for those who suffer from complexes about themselves, their educational levels, their afflictions (if any) to have the opportunity to be relieved of such complexes.

(vii) Literacy: The problems of illiteracy are always present with us and often neglected, ignored or concealed because they are not readily apparent. The need to tackle this problem is apparent.

(viii) Further Education and Training: Advice, encouragement and stimulation to undertake further education and training are an urgent necessity in order to preserve employment, to provide further opportunities, and to cater for those seeking to enter the workforce or those who are under-employed.

(ix)   Childcare: The facility to care for children of lone parents or women seeking to enter the workplace is apparent.

(x)   A Study Centre: There is a need to have a place for children living in disadvantaged domestic situations to be helped with homework and with study.

(xi)   Small Storage Depot: The Society of St Vincent de Paul has identified the need for such a depot to facilitate proper distribution of goods to the needy.

(xii) Environmental Awareness: There is a need to provide a greater awareness of the protection of the environment amongst the local population of young and not so-young.

(xiii) Home Management: There is a need to provide advice on home management.

(xiv) Entertainment: There is a need to provide traditional entertainment in the locality, with particular awareness of the elderly.

(xv)   Arts and Crafts Classes: There is a need to have such classes available, with particular emphasis on catering for the elderly and under-employed.

(xvi) Parenting Programme: A need exists among young parents in the community to provide a parenting programme that will help them to cope with the demands of raising a young family.

The overall objective of the Social Enterprise Programme is to provide a co-ordinating mechanism for projects that will facilitate the marginalised and disadvantaged sectors of the local area in becoming involved in using the facilities and schemes which will be provided within the total integrated programme of the development company.

22

Levels and Phases of Community Enterprise

To understand what I mean by levels of community enterprise, let us remove the aspect that is least organic — Built Environment Renewal. This leaves two options for examination — Social and Cultural Stimulation and Local Economic Innovation. These can best be explained by the "Higgins Matrix".

Matrix of Levels of Community Enterprise

	C Advanced SCS/ Retarded LEI	D Advanced SCS/ Advanced LEI
Social and Cultural Stimulation (SCS)	A Retarded SCS/ Retarded LEI	B Retarded SCS/ Advanced LEI

Local Economic Innovation (LEI)

It is quite obvious that the decision regarding the level at which any community enterprise plan is to be aimed must take cognisance of the above indicators of advancement. Any one of the above four positions can be found in local communities.

In terms of community enterprise, everything is relative — relative to the local advancement, relative to national indicators of development, relative to neighbouring towns and villages. No area can ever say that it has advanced to completion. Enterprise and development are organic processes.

In general, the advancement of Built Environment Renewal (BER) will relate to the state of positioning of the other two indicators. Poor BER will be found alongside Retarded SCS/ Retarded LEI. Advanced BER, however, can lie comfortably beside Retarded SCS/Advanced LEI but will generally not be found at the diagonally opposite corner of Advanced SCS/ Retarded LEI. In other words, as a general rule, Advanced BER is found close to Advanced LEI. So which of the three aspects of community development should be given priority?

An examination of the matrix will decide. In Kiltimagh, the advice from on high was to adopt a single project-by-project approach. It was the majority opinion of the Board of IRD Kiltimagh, however, that Kiltimagh needed a large boost of economic development and innovation. The town was dishevelled. The local economy was almost battered to death. The area needed to be brought back to its former glory. It needed to be made feel that it was as good as any other district in the region of comparable size. This could be called the "Defensive Innovation" stage. Kiltimagh was at point A on the matrix and trying to move towards point D.

Types of Innovation

To implement an economic miracle, the district and its planners, IRD Kiltimagh, were forced to take up the cudgel and implement a Defensive Innovation Programme. This aspect was almost completed in four years of work.

Implementing this phase of enterprise also meant allowing a fair degree of "Passive Innovation" to occur. The Passive Innovation stage is where someone has a gut-feeling that something will work. There is a large degree of chance (and often sentimentality) attached to its implementation. It is often the most dangerous stage with a large degree of risk — both business and financial — attached to its implementation.

The community that reaches points B or D on the matrix can afford largely to abandon the stages of Defensive and Passive Innovation and can move to the "Positive Innovation" stage, where the community adopts plans and projects for implementation that are different to what others are doing. The corner of the market, which Japanese entrepreneurs so avidly seek for their products, is at this point being sought after by the community planners. The community seeks to make its

area different from other areas and usually begins to define its
new position in terms of creating a distinct brand-image for
itself. The community has now firmly decided on the segment
of the marketplace that it is targeting for its products, and it
devises unique and innovative schemes to reach its goal.

Brand-Image

Kiltimagh, having gone through the phases of Defensive and
Passive Innovation, is now pursuing a vigorous Positive Innovation plan. It has decided to adopt the brand-image
"Kiltimagh — The Artisan Village". It will develop this image
in a structured way by encouraging and emphasising traditional aspects of economic and cultural development. Schemes
are being devised to encourage local craft workers to locate in
the area, to establish businesses, and to undertake training
programmes. Outside artisans and craft workers are being offered a range of incentives to locate in Kiltimagh. People of artistic talent are being similarly enticed to come and stay for a
while or to settle in Kiltimagh. Emphasis on community arts is
high on the agenda. Traditional forms of leisure and entertainment are being featured in pubs and during festivals. The
town has devised a bilingual programme to be implemented in
co-operation with Bord na Gaeilge.

Kiltimagh is no different from any other town or village in
Ireland. There is no reason why similar schemes cannot be
devised for these. Each of our towns and villages must once
again develop its own unique brand-image. It must strive to be
different. The blandness of our Irish towns and villages makes
most just "me too" towns. The odd town that has devised its
own unique features attracts attention and is thereby an attractive place in which to contemplate investment. These distinct and attractive features will instil confidence in locals to
invest and will attract outside investment. The result is an ex-
panding economic base.

How sad it is that only a few towns in Ireland spring to
mind in this category. The villages of Tyrellspass and Kilbeg-
gan, County Westmeath are a case in point. The County Cork
village of Rosscarbery is another example. How we all would
love to emulate the thematic approach to planning as shown in

the food gourmets' town of Kinsale or in County Mayo's lovely Westport. The notion that all these towns have to be seaside towns must be dispelled. Hence, I mention Westmeath villages and, of course, our own Kiltimagh must not be forgotten as an inland town with a thematic framework as a plan for development.

Phases of Community Enterprise

To understand community enterprise, there is one further feature that deserves examination. This third element — phases of community development — relates solely to the human resources working as volunteers to implement the plan.

The diagram below indicates some significant phases of "attitude changes" in the voluntary sector. There are many more. Some individuals in the voluntary workers sector go through fewer phases than indicated, while others experience many more extreme phases. One thing that is certain, however, is that crests and troughs will come. All businesses in the real world experience crests and troughs. The difference with crests and troughs in the world of community enterprise lies in the speed at which these phases are arrived at and gone through.

Phases of Community Enterprise

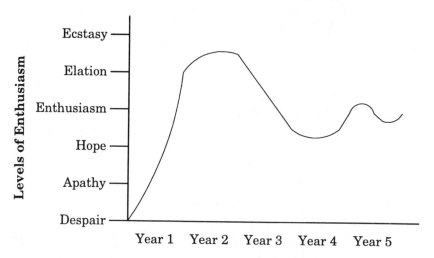

For some in the voluntary sector the troughs become unbearable, and the very first time that the "wall" is hit, resignations are in the air. Others are more resilient, but all will experience severe doubts. This is where the steadfastness of professional management must keep an even tiller. The lack of professional management can sound the death-knell of community enterprise where plans are abandoned in mid-stream at the first advancing trough.

The Crest ...

In September 1991, Kiltimagh's plan was judged as one of five regional winners of the ESB Community Enterprise Awards. The award ceremony for the presentation of the overall award was held in Galway and no one knew the winner, which was to be announced during dinner.

Representatives of all regional winners had beautiful display stands in the foyer of the banqueting hall in the Corrib Great Southern Hotel. Every device in the book was used by groups to try to find any significant indicators of advantage. Kiltimagh had the first stand inside the door — was this significant? Mountmellick was given ten extra tickets — was this a sign of a winner? Pat Collier of Macra na Feirme, who directed the programme, smiled at everyone — who got the best smile? One member of our group suggested that a tip to a waitress whom we knew might get her to take a peep in the adjoining press office. Through it all, the suspense was killing.

President Robinson arrived, followed by a battalion of photographers and television personnel. She seemed to accord equal time to each group. Still it was impossible to predict the winner. Hopes rose and fell like a seagull on the Sea of Erris. Come to think of it, maybe Erris had won? The chief executive of the ESB is Joe Moran, a Mayo man. Was this a positive or negative factor for the two Mayo entrants? Dunlewey had beautiful resources and looked lovely in photographs? Carlingford had been trying for a good while. I knew at first-hand that Mullingar had a good programme. Eventually the dinner plates were taken up and the awards ceremony got underway.

One by one, regional awards and merit awards were distributed. Our chairman, Brian Mooney, was amongst the regional recipients on behalf of Kiltimagh. Then, to a fanfare of trumpets, Joe Moran opened the envelope and Kiltimagh was called to receive an additional cheque for £50,000. Three years later, President Robinson told me that she still remembered the cheer from the Kiltimagh contingent.

The celebrations went on into the early morning. Interviews with press, radio and television had to be undertaken, whilst brandies were the order of the day. Nancy Lavin, a board member who doubled as our coach driver for the night, informed us that a torch-light welcome awaited us and that Kiltimagh town was "jammed".

Just as we were leaving Galway, one community member approached me to congratulate me for the tenth time and express supreme pride.

"Will you give us a guarantee of four more years? If you will, then the sky is the limit. Ask for what you want. We'll get it for you," he concluded.

And then we headed for the celebrations in Kiltimagh.

... the Trough ...

I tell this story to show the crest of the wave in September 1991. But by February 1992, projects in the plan had entered the slow, hard-slog stages. Bureaucracy had stalled some plans, while others were stalled for want of money.

The first trough had arrived. From crest to trough took exactly five months. My "the sky is the limit" benefactor of September was now seriously questioning IRD's efficiency. Others too were reflecting similar feelings.

... and How to Cope

I decided that it was time to press the "Recall" button. It is absolutely essential for all community enterprise managers to keep written and photographic evidence of "before" and "after" situations. Like the general public, board members have very short memories. They need to be reminded of how things used to be before the renewal started.

I decided, however, to keep the photographs and slides for a further trough. Instead I wrote ten questions to put to each board member as part of my report to the next meeting. As I drafted the questions, I wondered whether I would be asked to resign for being so daring.

Our chairman, Brian Mooney, was the first to react. He had read the questions over and over again and informed the board that he intended to keep them by his bedside as his "Bible" for whenever further doubts surfaced.

My questions were:

(i)   Have we the staying-power to see our plan to completion?

(ii)   Are we going to become a "me-too" company which changes tack in mid-stream and at a time when we most need to prove our resilience?

(iii)   Can we overcome the burn-out that is inevitable after a hectic two years of activity?

(iv)   Are we capable of continuously appraising our present position by comparison with the pre-IRD position?

(v)   Are we in danger of losing the freshness and enthusiasm that epitomised our earlier attitudes?

(vi)   Are we now satisfied with the small, slow results for our efforts which, in the initial stages, we would have been delighted with?

(vii)   Does the prospect of a continuous flow of visitors from educational institutions and community groups, both national and international, to hear of our efforts no longer excite us?

(viii) Do we take for granted the changing face of Kiltimagh and are we no longer proud of these changes?

(ix)   Are we on the alert for external jealousies of our success and determined not to allow these to destroy our efforts?

(x)   Are we strong enough to withstand the petty conflicts from within:

◊   The human feelings that our voluntary effort is putting money into the pockets of those who "never do anything" for the community

◊   The human feelings in our immediate family regarding our giving so much time to our community

◊   Our own innate feelings that we could very well do the job that those being paid salaries/wages in the company do

◊   Are we at conflict within ourselves that our community's money is being used to pay management and permanent staff?

◊   The public acknowledgement of management means that invitations and travel and social occasions are necessary. As we are the voluntary workers, how do we feel about our exclusion now and then from these occasions?

◊   Finally, do we realise that the crests and troughs of community development come faster than in any other business?

Any one of these answers could be vital in determining our attitude to our company and its activities, and ultimately in the success of our endeavours.

This concluded my questionnaire. We moved from the trough to the next crest without resignations — mine or anyone else's!

The subsequent crests and troughs during all community enterprise plans are always less pronounced and consequently less precarious than the potential tidal-wave consequences of the first trough.

23

Community Leadership

In 1968, Tannenbaum and Schmidt concluded that the style of leadership adopted reflects, and is contingent on, four variables:

(i)   The Leader — the personality and preferred styles of the leader

(ii) The Led — the needs, attitudes and skills of subordinates

(iii) The Task — the requirements and goals of the job to be done, i.e. the plan

(iv) The Context — The organisation being led and its values and prejudices.

I will endeavour to analyse community leadership in an Irish cultural context using these four variables.

The Leader

What makes one person a good community leader while others may never realise their ambition to lead? The answer to the question begs me to analyse the qualities of community leaders with whom I have worked over the past 25 years. To me, the following attributes must be present, to some degree or other, in all community leaders:

- They must be unselfish in their devotion to community service and be prepared to make sacrifices of their own time and money within reasonable limits.

- They must possess a love of, and be proud of, their own place. Without this, their negative vibes will destroy the confidence of others in development projects.

- They must have a certain arrogance and self-assurance about themselves and their own place and the role of both in the larger world. This gives them the ability to demand more from outsiders, and an assurance to demand better from the community being served.

- They must be capable of a large degree of objectivity in all situations.

- They must have, and be seen to have, personal integrity in their own lives.

- They must have a natural enthusiasm for community enterprise.

- They must naturally want to support, however tentatively, other community activities.

- In reflecting an image of their community, they must always want to present the best image.

- They should possess a fair degree of charisma. Very often this will combine with charm and wit.

- They must be personable and extroverted, yet prudent with language and conversation.

- They must not be always seeking the limelight, and instead should be willing to let the larger community or other volunteers take some of the praise, some of the time.

- They must never allow their party political leanings interfere with their objectivity.

- They must be democratic, while realising the inherent danger in over-reliance on democracy.

- They must be patient listeners

- They must have natural ability to organise.

- They must possess initiative and be capable of rousing enthusiasm so that others may follow their example.

- They must possess the "helicopter" trait — the ability to rise above a particular situation and see it in its broader context, and then to descend quickly and attend to the detail of getting the task underway and completed.

- Above all else, they must possess a vision for their community. Very often, this vision is unexpressed verbally and displays itself in other ways.

The Community Manager

My contention that all communities need professional management in order to plan strategically the development process
leads us to an analysis of the qualities needed in community
managers.

The first and absolute quality that every community manager must possess is that of being a positive thinker. When this
difficult vocation is chosen as a career path, the manager must
be prepared for all difficulties and for all disappointments. The
time-wasting aspect which attaches to the diplomacy that is
demanded, the troughs and crests, the apparent ingratitude of
snide remarks that seem to take no account of the long hours
given to the "vocation" are all part of the difficulties. Any tendency towards negativity will be reinforced in the difficult task
of working through a community plan with the voluntary sector, some of whom will probably be brimming with the arrogance of believing that only they know best for "their" community. The attitude that the manager is being paid to do all
community jobs will have to be challenged. The pace at which
disappointments come is an inevitable feature of the job also,
and consequently the need for a positive thinker is all the more
pertinent.

The ability to confront immediately all deviations from ac-
ceptable practice must be possessed in large measure. Im-
posing further restrictions or new impositions, or casting re-
flections on the personal integrity of management, must be
dealt with promptly and decisively. When the crunch comes,
the manager must make a stand against such behaviour. Allowing the wound of indignation to fester only prolongs the
fateful day. Managers who are doing the job as prescribed, and
often much more, should not abide any insults to their work or
character without making the appropriate objections to such
behaviour and at the proper level — generally to the chairperson, as leader of the organisation. This is where maturity is
called for on all sides, and is where younger managers can often resign in despair.

The ability to communicate well, both in writing and verbally, is another essential requirement for being effective. Well-
documented applications for assistance, report-writing and

filing, letters that are succinct yet self-explanatory are all steps along the way to the community manager becoming accepted as a competent, determined individual.

The ability to acknowledge support and assistance that has been given never goes astray. Every significant meeting, every bit of help given through advice or monetary assistance, every support document received through the mail should be duly acknowledged in writing. It costs very little and means so much to the giver. It also paves the avenue for further requests for help.

The ability to communicate verbally is another great asset for the community manager. Experience of public speaking or debating is invaluable because 90 per cent of the success of community management is about good presentation and communication. We must get the message across. Message-bearers should always assume that they are starting at the lowest common denominator — that their opposite number knows nothing of what is being explained, and hence the explanation must be given from the beginning, in a precise manner, without being diverted onto unrelated subjects.

Community managers must be analysts and strategists. Analysis of proposals both quickly and later with in-depth scrutiny is an essential part of their job. Similarly, the ability to devise strategy for project development is a must.

The manager who is both a visionary and a strategist has special qualities that should be rewarded and appreciated by community. Too often we find the visionary floating around in the sky while the strategist never leaves the ground. The combination of vision and strategy is the foundation for implementing the "helicopter" trait.

The quality of diplomacy has already been referred to and is one of those qualities that differentiates the community manager from the regular business manager. Service to community demands patience and diplomacy. Nevertheless, the ability to be forthright and confrontational, when necessary, must not be forgotten.

Coupled with diplomacy, discretion, confidentiality and street-wisdom are also called for in a competent community manager. When, and what, to report to the voluntary sector must be decided. Whom to meet, whom to avoid, and what to reveal to the general public are key decisions to be addressed.

The salary offered to a community manager will decide the quality of person the community gets to serve it. As the saying goes, "If you pay peanuts, you get monkeys". Restrictions on the ability of many communities to pay for community management means that often the best person cannot be bought in the marketplace. This in turn leads to poor morale within the organisation — knowing that you are "second-best" can be a starting point for failure. It is better for communities to manage their own affairs voluntarily, than to appoint managers who are chosen only because they are affordable.

The corollary of this is not that community managers must be local fund-raisers in order to pay for themselves. The community manager who must undertake the fund-raising task will have little respect and will more than likely "jump ship" at the first available opportunity. Local fund-raising is for the voluntary sector to undertake.

The maturity of the manager, when chosen, will be an important factor in ensuring that "burn-out" does not occur too soon. Invariably in community development, the point is reached by some where the volume of work they undertake leads to a point where burn-out occurs. The effects of burn-out are highly traumatic and while most recover, some push that inch too far and induce serious physical or mental illness from which full recovery is impossible. The "missionary aspects" of community development have all the "bacteria" required to bring about this dreadful state. A burnt-out manager is of little use to any community and hence the ability to pace oneself in a mature way and, more importantly, to be allowed to pace oneself, is vital.

The professional manager must also be self-effacing about success. While being entitled to revel in significant achievements, allowing these to interfere with the pace of other developments or to displace the work-rate must be avoided.

Related to this is the determination to avoid publicity for oneself and to allow as much credit as possible to go where it belongs — to the community, via community representatives who give voluntarily to the job-in-hand. Publicity-seeking by professional management can cause annoyance and cynicism in many circles, not least where it matters most within the context of the local community organisation. The realisation that it is the "community team" which forms part of all successes must be constantly borne in mind, when successes come. Nevertheless, this must be counterbalanced with the confidence in one's own ability to succeed.

Organisations should realise the need for professional management to be allowed "thinking time". This should not be confused with statutory holidays. To have the time study other systems, to network with others in the same line of work, to think and to reflect, or perhaps even just to have the time to write without interruption is an absolute essential. The refusal to allow such time to the competent manager leads to a less than effective response. The effects on home life of a hectic schedule should not be forgotten in this context.

Finally, from personal experience, the manager must have a wardrobe for all seasons. Professional management means dressing professionally at all times. I am a great believer in good personal presentation as being one of the factors in commanding respect. Well-dressed people can have a huge edge on opponents, in negotiations or in brokerage. Subconsciously, the standard of dress and a neat appearance do make a difference and can eventually be the influencing factor for success. Professional dressing relates to being professionally paid. The poorly paid manager with large personal overheads can hardly be expected to sport the best-branded suits. A wardrobe for all events and seasons is the perfect balance.

The Led

Community comprises many different styles of people and groups. There are voluntary organisations in the community with their own sectoral interests. Some, but not all, of the members of these groups will probably also want to be part of any larger community enterprise initiative.

The voluntary sector includes: the apathetic, the sympathetic, the "too grand to notice", the "too poor to care", the "been there, done that" old guard, the enthusiastic, the visionaries, the artistic, the socially-minded, the business person, the entrepreneur, the idealists, the liberals, the unemployed, the unskilled and the skilled.

In preparing a community enterprise plan and in establishing our "context" or organisation, we must take account of the needs and desires of most of these. Nothing will happen, however, if we go over-board on democracy and wait for maximum participation. Experience shows that a small handful of people will eventually be the workers to undertake the projects and see the plan to completion.

The National Pastime

No other single factor impedes the "bottom-up" development and expression of communities more than the national pastime of begrudgery.

What is the essence of begrudgery? I believe that it is to be found in envy. But begrudgers verbalise their envy. Begrudgers subconsciously hate to see their neighbours being successful in business or having a lucky streak. They celebrate success in the midst of all, and then slink to the back of the pub to drop the odd, and carefully selected, clanger, to start the gossip that will destroy the victor.

The effects of the national pastime are everywhere to be seen, with particular effects in small rural communities and towns and villages. It is easier to become a "hurler on the ditch" than to take part in the fray. People, and the young in particular, are terrified of starting their own businesses or of trying to develop an innovative idea because of the deadly venom of begrudgery. Community activists shirk from taking leadership roles because of the known presence of the sniping of the critics who are steeped in begrudgery. Perhaps the success of our exiles is that they can go on to realise their full potential when released from the risk of the begrudgers' tongues.

What can be done to alleviate the effects of begrudgery on community enterprise? The first step must be to change attitudes via our educational system. To inspire an enterprise culture, we must first seek an independent, courageous and positive-thinking generation.

The courage to try, the ability to succeed, and the determination to beat the begrudger is vital as we endeavour to bring our country and particularly community enterprise out of the dark ages of dependency.

The Task

The task to be undertaken is contained in the plan, which must reflect the long-term vision of the community. It will go further in reflecting the methods to be used to focus on and to implement that vision.

The Vision

The vision should be expressed in answer to the questions:

- Where do you wish to see this community in 20 years' time?
- What do you wish for this community?
- What type of community would you like to be part of in 20 years' time?
- What type of community and area would the next generation want to inherit?

The Focus

In endeavouring to focus on implementation, the first requirement is to prepare a Mission Statement. This statement (preferably no longer than a single sentence) seeks to encapsulate the global concept to be included in the task of planning. For instance, a mission statement for a particular community could read:

> Our Community (name) has as its primary objective to promote the economic, cultural and social development of the (name) region by way of integrated and managed internal planning, in a way that will protect and dynamically enhance the environment, heritage and population.

Sectoral Programmes

The next requirement in planning is to decide the sectoral aspects of the plan. The planners must decide on the sectors from among the common programme areas of:

(i) Environment — Built (Infrastructural) and/or Natural

(ii) Social

(iii) Economic — Tourism; Agriculture (main-stream, alternative, agri-tourism); Commercial (services, manufacturing, telematics).

Each programme should be analysed and decisions arrived at regarding:

(i)   The main objective

(ii)   The specific objectives.

So far we can assume that the planners have avoided the task of deciding the core of the process that incorporates the area of strategic planning. Strategic planning occurs in the context of specific projects and will evolve as follows.

Once the selection of sectoral programmes has been completed, the task of choosing "likely" projects must be undertaken. This task is not as easy as at first appears and the process is likely to cause considerable debate once the realisation of the three- or four-year commitment to these specifics becomes apparent. The discipline of focus is not an easy one to achieve. The projects chosen will then be analysed and documented under a series of headings including the essentials:

- Background — placing the project in its context
- Objective — specific to this project
- Strategies — step-by-step approach to the task
- Timescale — preferably a maximum of two years
- Budgets — both capital costs and funding sources, with an operational budget for each project where larger expenditures are in question.

The fear in most community activists of having to undertake the foregoing planning process is understandable. There is an unspoken dread of endeavouring to document a four-line or 100-line idea into a full written work. There is the alternative dread of having to pay a consultant to co-ordinate ideas and having to spend community money to do it. Nevertheless, it cannot be stated too clearly that the presentation of a well-researched plan to any funding source, either banks or state agencies, makes the case for planning much easier. This salient point must not be dismissed lightly. In the absence of a good community scribe, the harsh reality of hiring outside help should be faced.

Sometimes, however, the cost of outside help can be reduced

considerably where community activists undertake the research and documentation of the statistical analysis that grounds the plan in a specific community context.

The following check-list should be worked through by community activists and will alleviate much of the research to be charged for by a consultant:

Support Document for Community Enterprise Applications:

- Abstract — The overall context in which the plan is being prepared and the main arguments for its advancement. This will not be in great detail and very often can be written as the last item for inclusion at the start of the completed plan.
- Proposers' Background — The group's history and individual members' profiles.
- Profile of the Community and District — Specific advantages or disadvantages; political boundaries; population base of the town and rural district; changes in the population; intercensal variation per rural district and urban centres in the area; details of the commercial and industrial base from previous studies (strengths and weaknesses); significant players in sustaining the local economy; industrial and commercial history and current analysis; access and transport systems; land use and structure; employment; other economic activities.
- Project Proposal — Briefly describe the project.
- Project Background — Describe where the project arose from.
- Project Objectives(s) — What exactly does the community want from this project?
- The Market (potential and actual).
- The Implementation Process — What is the step-by-step approach for progressing this project?
- Budgetary Implications — What funds or other benefits-in-kind (for example, a site or office) will be forthcoming from the proposers or from other sources for this project?
- Other Supporting Details — For example, educational and training facilities; recreational and entertainment facilities

and amenities; social and community interaction; SWOT analysis of the area.

The Context

The preparation of an Action Plan for community enterprise cannot be done to an inflexible pre-set formula. The individual characteristics of each community and the resources within it are the vital ingredients for successful community enterprise. The initial resource audit of the community will reveal the human and physical skills and resources that are available.

Planning in this context should begin on the basis of working to a model of development such as the Keynes Econometric model which emphasises the internal producer and consumer elements, combined with government interventions and their role in networking with the outside world.

The Higgins Matrix, in which I have endeavoured to show the levels of community enterprise, will decide the context within which the task of community enterprise can be set.

At this point, let me sound a note of caution. Over-emphasis on local economics as the only future engine for growth frightens me. There is a tendency to regard local economics as the tool to solve national economic problems such as the failure to convert high economic growth into high job-creation figures. While local economics should be the essential driving force, it should not be seen as a panacea for all our problems. The development of sound, vibrant local economics capable of participating in global economics is the answer. To neglect either factor is to repeat the mistakes of the economic history of this country, which saw local economics ignored for far too long.

Finally, the context in which an action plan for community enterprise is set will be decided by the roles that members of the community need to play, or are capable of playing, in the whole process. To prescribe actions that are beyond the potential of a community to implement is a stupid exercise. To prescribe actions for which there is little enthusiasm or willingness in a community is no less stupid.

Recognising the potential of the context is the bedrock of what is achievable in community enterprise.

24

Local Money and Local Politics

In actively pursuing many sources of funds for the Kiltimagh development programme, the single most active ingredient in making a successful case for help was being able to tell the story of how a small population base of about 2,500 people (including a small town of 1,000) had determined that, if it were a question of money, their town was going to be saved from the annihilation of economic decline.

Local Money

As is revealed elsewhere in this book, the local community in Kiltimagh made direct cash subscriptions over a four-year period of approximately £28,000 per annum. The pinnacle of this direct method of funding was in the first year. Armed solely with a Company Prospectus, which was really only a "wish list", the twenty or so voluntary collectors called door-to-door throughout the area seeking a direct cash subscription from each wage-earner of £2.50 per week or £9 per month or £100 per year at a minimum. The commitment was sought for a four-year period.

Some refused but, as the figures reveal, most rallied to the cause. "Would you not think that to save Kiltimagh is worth giving the price of two pints of Guinness per week?" was the type of simple economics presented to reluctant subscribers. My experience in other communities has shown that it is usually the ones who question most and who are most reticent in committing themselves that eventually are the most loyal.

Ask First, Build Later

The foregoing is an important lesson for community groups contemplating this direct funding route. Most will argue that "we have to build the community centre — we have to show some proof before we can ask". The Kiltimagh experience discounts this argument and shows that, before you start seriously to identify and focus on any project, you can go to your community selling nothing more than hope, provided that you have a credible group of people with a credible and cohesive argument.

The important point here is that you are not asking for direct funding for the community centre or the football pitch, which are single projects. Instead you are asking for funding towards a process that will provide for the development of numerous projects. The project-by-project approach has killed the real development potential of communities. I believe that community activists are 80 per cent oriented towards projects and only 20 per cent towards the processes to achieve integrated planning, involving a series of projects.

The single project will swallow up all the funds and, too often, the goodwill of community funding sources. "Sure, we subscribed towards the GAA centre two years ago." "Sure, we have no one at home any longer to use that place." "Sure, all our crowd had to go to England, there was never anything for them here." These are the reasons invariably used for refusal. The only rebuttal that can be used for these very true-to-reason arguments is an appeal to see that this is a different approach. It is a different way of doing things. It is a new beginning of a whole new process.

This appeal, to the in-built pride-of-place in the vast majority of people must be a large part of the argument for getting support. An appeal to rely on the collector's good name and reliability will generally seal the argument: "You never saw me doing this before. I'm doing it because things are so bad. I'm doing it because I believe we have one last chance to save this place. You know me for years and I guarantee you that when my name is attached to this effort, I will be the first one to cry 'halt' if it appears to be wasting money."

The alternative method, and one usually suggested by communities, is to start a single project and then to ask. I believe that, in doing this, you are back to the project-by-project approach. You are nailing your colours to one mast, and the whole process for the potential of the multiplier effect can be lost.

Of course it takes courage, a lot of courage, to go to a neighbour's door and ask for funding. If it were easy, it would be happening in every community every year.

Why Should We Contribute?

So why should communities have to be philanthropic? Why should they have to give money to get projects developed in their locality? The state has a moral duty to provide these things.

"There is plenty of money there. We pay our taxes and I'm damned if I'll pay any more for any development process" goes the argument. I dispute this argument on a number of grounds.

First, as long as all communities rely on someone "up there" to do it for us or to send an offer of the money, it will never happen. We must go after the money and the schemes that are available.

Second, we must capture the niche in the state assistance market, using the spirit of self-help and helping others. It is nothing more than an extension of the traditional "meitheal" system, whereby neighbour helped neighbour during harvesting times. Manpower was the unit of currency of self-help then, money by way of local support is the replacement unit of the meitheal now.

Third, the fact that we are no longer just going with the begging-bowl to ask, but are showing our own commitment to the local development process, distinguishes our community from the next. It shows our willingness to be involved, and it shows our determination to succeed.

Direct and Indirect Funds

The reader may have observed my insertion of the adjective "direct" throughout the last few pages. I did so in order to help us to distinguish between direct and indirect funding. In diagrams following, we see the effects of direct local funding contrasted with those of indirect local funding. The ideal method is to employ both funds.

In Kiltimagh, we called direct funds the "Core Fund". The core fund is the capital for implementation of the enterprise process. The principle is that every effort should be made to avoid depletion of this core fund below the figure of the first year's subscription. In other words, £40,000 is regarded as a reserve fund. If this fund became depleted, the panic button would be pressed.

Indirect funds, on the other hand, were known as the "Biscuit-Tin" Fund, probably because of the association with the most commonly-used item for collecting these funds. This fund is the community's contributions towards the implementation of specific projects. Indirect funds can be raised by the usual methods — raffles, dances, lotteries, race nights, novelty events, etc. The list is endless and the ingenuity of local communities in devising innovative methods of fund-raising never ceases to amaze me.

The effects of the core fund in comparison to the biscuit-tin fund are almost self-explanatory. The multiplier effect which both funds have deserves examination. So too do the trigger effect and the sense of permanence.

The Multiplier Effect

When IRD Kiltimagh began to emerge as a development force in the community, the concept of the multiplier effect was explained by Philip Mullally of the IRD Trust. He explained that money raised locally for a process would be matched by his organisation. He emphasised that the project-by-project approach would not receive funds from this source.

Nevertheless, a one-to-one multiplier was on offer. He further explained that the process could, and would, receive funds and benefits-in-kind by way of advice from other sources in the private sector. Finally, as individual development projects were proposed and advanced, state funds available would create a further multiplier. In all, he predicted a multiplier of 3:1 per annum on funds raised locally.

In our first full period of audited figures, the multiplier effect generated in this way by IRD Kiltimagh was in excess of 7:1.

The Trigger Effect

As projects are advanced for start-up, the single biggest obstacle is the need to have funds to start. Each state agency will need to see proof of matching funds, the banks will want someone else to start the process, and generally stalemate is reached. This is where the trigger effect of the local fund is essential. In IRD Kiltimagh, we used the core fund to give that initial boost to a project when stalemate was the only alternative.

The principle behind this triggering was the clear understanding that the money was a "loan" to the project. The core fund was the provider of a revolving loan, without which few, if any, projects would ever have started.

The Effect of the "Core Fund" in Comparison to the "Biscuit-Tin Fund"

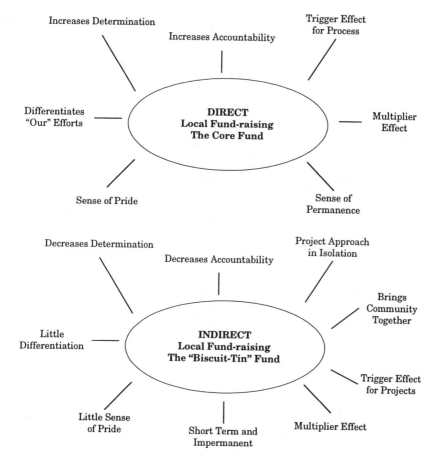

The Sense of Permanence

The core fund provides this necessary sense of permanence. Where communities rely on the biscuit-tin fund, the impermanence of community enterprise is felt. The fact that impermanence has detrimental effects cannot be over-emphasised. Our centralised system of government does not provide for this sense of permanence in local enterprise. A project-by-project and time-limited approach is advocated from on high as the only method.

The need for the local community to know that the community office will not be gone next year is vital. The death-knell of so many community initiatives has been sounded by impermanence. Managers were appointed, office staff employed and then the funding ran out, leaving nothing but half-finished projects and a shattered community effort.

This problem must be addressed now and realistically if Government and the EU are really serious about rural renewal and local enterprise. Every single community that is willing to produce a viable economic and social plan, and is willing to provide adequate matching funds locally, must be given global support, not on a scheme-by-scheme and project-by-project basis, but on a permanent global-fund guarantee.

What enraged me most was that, while the laurels were being piled on us in IRD Kiltimagh from on high, my Chairman continuously had to wonder where the next penny would come from to ensure that he could keep management and a successful enterprise process in place. Where would the next scheme come from? Which begging-bowl would we use next? It is a dreadful indictment of Government that, in an age when lip-service is paid daily to local development, successful models like IRD Kiltimagh are being strangled by the very system that purports to have a serious policy on local development. It is time that the silent revolution of communities exposed this charade.

Local Politics

I honestly believe that the destruction of many community enterprise initiatives, or their failure to reach full potential, can be attributed to the immersion of some groups or sections of groups in local party politics. This stems from their blind determination to "serve the party first and community enterprise after". This just does not work, as my experience of travelling around to other communities, coupled with my experience in Kiltimagh, confirms.

Unless our political party activists are intelligent enough to reverse the equation, and put community enterprise as a definite first, community enterprise and rural renewal in Ireland are doomed to failure.

Perhaps an example will illustrate this: I was invited as the main guest speaker to deliver a talk on tourism development to a community organisation in an area which has so many beautiful and natural resources that it is almost criminal not to allow others to benefit from, and enjoy, them. The area has such potential that it is crying out for an enterprising approach to produce a quality tourism experience there.

My talk and the meeting were well-publicised in advance. In reading the pre-meeting publicity, I observed that one notice for the meeting contained reference to one local politician, while another notice contained almost similar information but had reference to another local politician. Strange to say, they were both members of the same political party.

As soon as I arrived at the door of the meeting-place, I was greeted by one of these politicians. He emphasised his role in organising the meeting and decried the efforts of "others who jumped on the bandwagon". Before I reached the podium, I was accosted by the second politician, only to hear almost the same message.

I had had enough. In the course of my talk, I entered the dangerous arena of local politics, and I decried the detrimental effect this was having on the enterprise process there. Needless to say, I was never invited back. Needless to add, the same community group is still floundering.

Keep Politics out of Community Enterprise

I have the utmost respect for politicians and for our political and democratic systems. In fact, the loyalty of politicians in assisting us with our development programmes in Kiltimagh is a constant source of genuine comment by me. When officialdom has failed to allow a good plan or scheme to proceed, which indeed has been rare enough (provided that previous schemes were well administered or that a scheme was vital to the development plan), then, and only then, have communities had to enlist the aid of their politicians. When that aid was enlisted in Kiltimagh, politicians from all political parties were absolutely and totally loyal to the cause of development.

This problem, which must be addressed by our politicians and others, is vital to the success of community enterprise. How do we ensure that local politics, with all the jealousies, dislikes, suspicions and, in some cases, hatred engendered by party differences, is removed from community enterprise without destroying the democratic systems which local activists feel it is their duty to support?

I believe that you can achieve this despite what seems an impossible task. The local activists of the largest parties — Fianna Fáil and Fine Gael — have been more than helpful to IRD Kiltimagh. Politicians of all parties have been exceptionally helpful and amenable, when needed. I have always been confident that all parties were available to help to organise meetings with Local Authorities, Government Ministers or European Commission staff. This, more than anything else, is the single most important feature for the success of community enterprise and cannot be over-emphasised.

From local activist, to local authority representative, to Teachta Dála, all must accept the independence of the community enterprise process and the real patriotism that is attached to serving the community and allowing communities to develop without playing party politics.

Finally, it must be noted that, in Kiltimagh, a lobby group was established with three representatives from each political party. These did excellent work in lobbying effectively for county councillors' allocations for improvements at places such as the Market Square. Members of the lobby group have always been available to me informally and have been most forthcoming when assistance was requested. Long may local politics survive by allowing enterprise to progress unhindered, with the minimum of interference but with the maximum of support.

25
A Different Way of Thinking

In August 1992, the second Kiltimagh Forum on development was held and was addressed by Mary O'Rourke TD, then Minister for Trade. The theme was "Looking Up for Jobs".

The first such forum, held in May 1991, had been entitled "Rural Communities — Survival". The guest speaker on that occasion was the then EU Commissioner, Ray McSharry.

The principle behind these fora was to provide an opportunity for debate in a unique manner. Most fora are top-down events with those on high reading papers and imparting knowledge. The Kiltimagh Forum took a radically different approach — local leaders were asked to read papers while those on high were invited to listen. Some Government Department officials, when first invited, were sceptical. Guarantees of protection by the chair were not much consolation. The radically different style of debate worried them. To the credit of most Departments, representatives were well disposed to listening. The one exception was the Department of Agriculture which refused to attend the first forum.

On the theme of "Looking Up for Jobs", I was mandated by my community to prepare and deliver a paper on a concept that I had evolved while trying to come to terms with the wide-ranging facets of development that were being employed in Kiltimagh. I asked a working group member and well-known local thinker, Michael Laffey, to assist. Michael Laffey and Joe Kelly (Business Manager, IRD Kiltimagh) worked diligently in writing the details of a concept about which I could not be objective because of my intense involvement in the process.

Below is reproduced the content of the paper produced by all three of us for this forum. Some minor amendments have been made arising from more recent experiences.

The concept of the "televillage" covered the perceived needs for real local enterprise to be developed. As the realisation of the need for a social development programme became apparent in IRD Kiltimagh, the differentiation of the economic and social enterprise programmes also became apparent. Accordingly, I have added the social enterprise programme to the televillage programme in order to marry the two vital elements of social enterprise and economic enterprise.

Proposal for Development Organisations in the Format of Televillages

Introduction

IRD Kiltimagh Limited is, at present, implementing a corporate plan. This plan classifies possible enterprise developments within its area of operation under three broad headings:

- Business enterprises set up by the company or by individuals or small groups of entrepreneurs. The motivation of the people involved is the development of a viable, profitable business. The projects proposed cover all sectors: agriculture, food, manufacturing, tourism, craft, service and information technology.

- Enterprises proposed and initiated by local people but which will need an input of venture capital in order to bring the projects to fruition. A wide range of possible projects has been discussed, again covering a large number of sectors.

- Environmental/infrastructural projects funded principally from public sources with some local contribution. While dealing with projects, both in the planning stage, and later, in the set-up and early-implementation stages, the company has become acutely aware of the need for a range of support facilities and expertise which must be provided if projects are to succeed.

In order that local economic activity can successfully take place in rural and other disadvantaged communities, a number of facilities and aids must be available:

- A scheme of financial incentives in order to enable projects to start and grow

- A physical location with facilities for the establishment of small businesses and manufacturing projects

- Human resources in the shape of the expertise needed to appraise, plan, develop and assist in the ongoing management and direction of projects.

The first two facilities have, in many cases, been provided:

- Schemes are now in place, which provide financial assistance for enterprise projects.

- Many community groups involved in economic development and employment creation now have physical resources such as enterprise centres.

- Provision of the third requirement has not yet been addressed to any great extent.

These human and managerial resources are vital for a number of reasons:

- Many of the proposers of projects have little or no previous experience in the type of enterprises that they are developing.

- This lack of specific training and managerial experience needs to be overcome by providing advisory and support services.

- The entrepreneur must know that help will be available when and where it is needed. This allows energy to be devoted to the management and development of the project.

- Projects encouraged, fostered and aided by rural enterprise companies have a requirement for all the inputs of advice and expertise needed by commercial enterprises in more developed locations.

- The need for professional advice and guidance, in these cases, is much greater than in established companies where there is already a reservoir of experience and expertise.

- Among many potential entrepreneurs, the perception of providers of services from distant, urban areas is that "they can tell us what to do but they are unwilling to live or have a business here because they believe that it would fail". This leads to a lack of confidence and trust in such providers.

- The help must be available where it can be seen. The manager must be able to discuss problems, face to face, with people who live and work in the same environment. This discussion must be with people whom they know, and who are seen to be committed to their advancement.

Lack of self confidence is recognised as one of the major constraints to development in disadvantaged areas. In order to stimulate this confidence, the services and expertise needed to help develop, operate and control enterprises must be available locally. The provision of these services, through a community enterprise company, would constitute a "televillage".

A televillage is a local community enterprise office, working with action-led business expertise and product-development systems, using modern business and telematics networks, provided within the area of operation of the company. There is an assumption, common among those who should know better, that, somehow, small businesses in disadvantaged areas do not need the supports that are regarded as vital to large developed enterprises in much more favourable locations. More, not fewer, services are needed. They must be provided where they are needed. If they are not, then people should not be surprised when many viable projects fail.

Requirements of a Successful Development Unit

Physical Location

Every development company must have a physical location containing office space, interview space, space for shop-front/office enterprises and space for manufacturing/service projects. This location is the visible sign of the presence of the company in the community and is the tangible assurance that the possibility of development is real.

The Televillage: Organisation of Services to Projects/Businesses

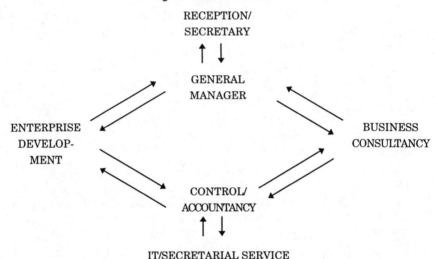

The Televillage: Interaction of Client and Services

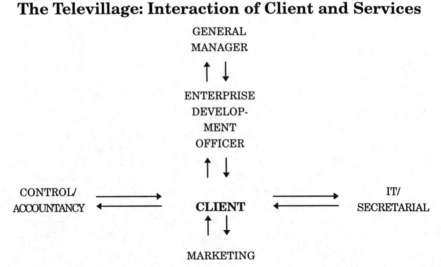

The Televillage: Reporting Structure of Development Unit

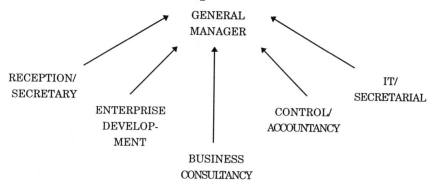

Reception / Secretarial Service

The centre must be staffed at all times. This is necessary to conduct normal business and to boost the confidence of those who deal with the company. It provides a definite, permanent point of contact which is always available to those who have business to transact.

Enterprise Co-ordinator / General Manager

The enterprise company must have a person to act in this capacity. He/she is the primary promoter of development and overall manager of the company. He/she is the initial source of information, advice and encouragement to those with development proposals and ideas. When a project provider approaches the televillage, the General Manager assesses the project and, if the project has merit, it should be referred to an Enterprise Officer (EO). The manager has responsibility for the overall direction of the company. He/she must continue to take an overview of its progress and respond to changing circumstances by developing and changing its focus and direction in the light of changing circumstances and opportunities. He/she must keep the board of the company, and the community fully informed and respond to enterprising initiatives from within the community.

Enterprise Officer(s)

The EO works within the televillage. The EO's brief is to research a proposed project and, together with other resource people as detailed later in this submission, prepare an overall, tailor-made package which makes the project viable and which will maximise its chances of succeeding and creating sustainable employment. As the scope of the company grows, more enterprise officers (EOs) will be needed for specific sectors. These people have specific responsibility for the development of project proposals which may be considered for aid by the board of the company. Their duties will be:

- To investigate the technical, financial and commercial feasibility of projects
- To investigate the availability of financial and technical assistance for the establishment of projects
- To establish the training needs of the managers and staff involved in projects
- To act as a link between the proposer(s) and state agencies in the development of projects
- To initiate and assist in product/service development for the projects
- To monitor the performance of projects and to act as a link between project managers and state and other agencies
- To act as the enterprise company's continuing point of contact for projects, reporting to the General Manager as required.

As the demand for services increases, EOs may specialise in particular sectors. A successful enterprise company needs at least three EOs, each specialising in development within specific sectors, as follows:

- Agriculture/Food
- Tourism
- Industry/Services.

Business Counselling

This is one of the key elements in the development of successful projects and for the development of sound, profitable businesses. It has two separate, but connected and interdependent, functions. Staff in the counselling service will:

- Appraise projects and assist in the initial, set-up phase by:
  ◊ Developing and providing a business plan and cash-flow projections for the new business
  ◊ Researching and keying into existing sources of funds
  ◊ Assisting project managers and proposers in negotiations with sources of commercial finance and venture capital
  ◊ Providing management expertise and advice where this is lacking
  ◊ Identifying possible niches in the market for the product or service
  ◊ Quantifying the niches identified
  ◊ Arranging the test marketing of the product/service where possible
  ◊ Formulating a marketing plan to cover the methodology of marketing the product/service
  ◊ Co-ordinating product development where necessary.
- Monitor, control and assist in the development and running of businesses at the request of their owners and/or the televillage by:

◊ Ensuring that businesses achieve budgetary, production and marketing targets

◊ Identifying and proposing appropriate, timely, remedial action where targets are not being met

◊ Providing accurate, relevant, up-to-date assessments of businesses from financial and management accounts

◊ Providing management with an early warning system by identifying any problems highlighted in the business accounts.

◊ Making businesses aware of changing trends and developing prospects in the market

◊ Providing the General Manager and Enterprise Officer with information on, and analysis of, the projects and businesses in their area of responsibility.

Information Technology / Secretarial Services

The development of an IT/secretarial service within the televillage will provide projects and developing businesses with the communications and information services which they need. This is vital in a situation where, by definition, businesses are remote from large centres of population and, in many cases, from their largest potential markets. The provision of such a service in a competent efficient form will go a long way in helping to overcome the worst disadvantages of remoteness. This service will be organised so that it provides services both internally and externally:

• Internally — Provide a secretarial, VAT, tax deduction, payroll, data transmission, information and communication service for:

◊ The General Manager and all other televillage staff

◊ Projects and businesses within the televillage and other company-sponsored projects. This will allow those involved in projects to concentrate on the management of their businesses without, at least initially, incurring the expense of providing all their own services. It provides them with a state-of-the-art, professional service which will help them to develop their business and lessen the penalty associated with any perceived remoteness. It will provide the necessary training and back-up for administrative staff when they decide to recruit their own.

◊ The business counselling service, by processing the data necessary for it to fulfil its function, acting as a data bank and communications centre, preparing presentations for its clients and customers, producing printed materials for submission to financial institutions, statutory and regulatory bodies.

• Externally — The facilities and expertise will be available to businesses and enterprises on a fee-paying basis. It will:

◊ Make available all the services which are available internally, to local businesses and enterprises

◊ Engage in training in the use of information technology

◊   Act as an information centre for dissemination of material available through electronic mail, EU, national data bases and bulletin boards.

Proposal

- That it be recognised that a major constraint to economic development in rural, and other disadvantaged areas, is the lack of available expertise in the stimulation, management and control of business enterprises.

- That funds be made available to IRD and other community-based organisations, the principal aim of which is enterprise development, to allow them to employ people with the required skills and expertise.

- That personnel covered by the scheme include Enterprise Officers, persons with expertise in Marketing, Business Management/Financial Planning and Control, in Information Technology, and persons with other expertise, the requirement for which can be clearly shown, and justified, on a case-by-case basis.

- A prerequisite for the appointment of a person to a position under this scheme is that they have a deep and abiding commitment to community enterprise development.

- The overall aim of the programme is to allow community enterprise organisations to acquire the expertise necessary to stimulate and assist economic development and employment within their area of operation.

- In the long term, the personnel employed will become largely, if not wholly, self-financing through the successful enterprises which they help to establish becoming their fee-paying clients.

- Where enterprise programmes are successful, these services will develop into separate businesses. This will make available sources of local expertise, which will make a significant contribution to local economies. They will also be a significant contribution to sustainable employment in their own right.

- At that stage, the parent development body will have a contractual arrangement with the business(es) to provide the services which they formerly provided as employees.

- That there be a requirement that the business(es) retain a fundamental commitment to economic development and remain located in the operational area of the development unit from which they have grown.

Suggested Outline of Scheme

- That funds be made available for the employment of skilled personnel by the televillage, or other qualifying community-based groups which apply, and which show a genuine need for expertise in the fulfilment of their role in economic development.

- That each application be accompanied by a fully documented case establishing:

    ◊   The type of personnel needed

◊ The number of personnel needed

◊ The current work load, the number and functions of existing personnel

◊ The type and range of work to be undertaken by the personnel applied for, and the subsequent reorganisation of functions, if any, within the unit.

• That where the need for the personnel requested has been established, the funds to allow appointment for a period of three years be allocated, subject to annual review.

• That an annual report be provided by the development unit showing:

◊ The work undertaken by each grant-aided employee

◊ The extra employment/monetary output generated or the progress achieved in project development

◊ The amount of fees/payments generated by each grant-aided employee.

Pilot Programmes

• It is proposed that the scheme be tested, and its feasibility and value proven, by introducing a series of pilot programmes immediately, as providing a sub-county structure to emerging County Enterprise Partnerships working with but independent of these. In other words, the principle of subsidiarity will apply.

• It is proposed that three locations in urban areas and three locations in rural areas be chosen. The primary criterion for picking these areas would be that they are already successfully involved in economic activity, with strong community support.

• Based on the experience of IRD Kiltimagh Limited, it is estimated that an annual budget would be as follows:

◊ Each Enterprise Officer (EO) will cost £20,000 in salary and associated sundry costs per year.

◊ Extra administration costs — £20,000 per year for the first EO to be employed, £15,000 for the second and £12,000 for the third and subsequent appointments.

◊ A provision of £40,000 in seed capital should be made available at the initiation of the project.

◊ It is assumed that a General Manager is already employed by the company and that the required secretarial support has been provided.

• Funding for the pilot projects should be shared by a number of sources. The suggested breakdown is as follows:

◊ Local community sources and private trusts: 25 per cent

◊ Central funds, public, employers and semi-state bodies: 75 per cent.

It is felt that the public, employers and semi-state bodies should be involved in the funding of EOs as they function in their area of competence. In other words, an EO who would be involved exclusively in tourist development projects should have a large proportion of his/her funding provided by Bord Fáilte; one who is involved exclusively in agriculture/food projects, by Teagasc and so on. In the initial stages, before specialisation is justified, funding can be shared among the agencies. The experience gained can be fully documented and made available to the agencies as a means of improving the range and effectiveness of their services.

- The agencies to be involved in the funding include Teagasc, FÁS, Bord Fáilte, CERT, Forbairt, County Enterprise Boards and Area Partnership Companies.

Development of a Social Programme through Resource Centres

The pro-active and directional style of management required for local economic activity is radically different from the facilitative style of management required for the development of a social enterprise programme. The debate over the urgency for a social enterprise programme versus an economic enterprise programme will continue to rage and is a matter of opinion based on your perspective.

The further debate as to which should come first in a list of priorities of community needs is also dependent on a number of non-quantifiable factors. Ideally the televillage concept will tackle both the social and economic needs in an integrated and concurrent way as outlined previously.

The following illustrates the two main physical location requirements for an ideal televillage development.

The Televillage: Physical Location Requirements

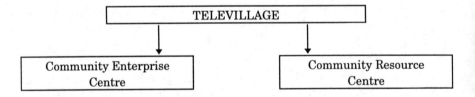

Able and Willing

The need for an appropriate and suitable physical location for a Social Enterprise Programme is apparent. The location and its ambience must be relaxed, non-threatening and non-inhibitive to the many strands of marginalised and socially alienated people and groups who need pro-active support. The specific support projects which are activated within this centre, and the physical development of the centre depend on the perceived needs of each specific community.

The needs as identified by IRD Kiltimagh for "An Tríú

Céim" are specified in Chapter 21. Finally, many enterprising communities are categorised either as being socially minded or economically minded. Unfortunately, the word enterprise has mistakenly come to be the prerogative of the latter group, whereas the real meaning of enterprise is "a willingness to start projects". The latter group must realise that for real economic and social enterprise to flourish, the social agenda must also be addressed. The need to fortify the capacity of our community to survive and the need to stimulate the latent capacity of our community to be enterprising must be included in the total community agenda. The ability of any community to retain or regain its vibrancy is dependent on both enterprising factors being interlinked.

26
Decentralisation

It is appropriate to remind ourselves once again of the real malaise of centralisation. Creeping centralisation has continued by stealth, despite the lip-service commitment to decentralisation. The move towards increased emphasis on global economics, with a concurrent decrease in emphasis on micro-economic development as a result of centralisation, has had a detrimental effect on rural Ireland, and on the West of Ireland in particular. Over the past 15 years, the move has been towards bigger businesses in bigger centres, with little regard for the needs of small businesses, and particularly for the needs of the service sector as a job provider.

Centralisation results in a loss of local identity, which eventually leads to a loss of confidence and of self-worth. The ultimate result of centralisation is the creation of a dependency culture and increasing state intervention. This is what must be tackled and ended. A pro-active policy of real decentralisation must be undertaken. This must not only relate to the decentralisation of large sectors of state departments, although much more could be done in this regard. It means that the whole mind-set of centralisation must be changed. It means that micro-aspects of Departmental work must be decentralised to small towns and villages. Despite arguments to the contrary, there is no proof that this would lead to inefficiency. In an age of modern telecommunications, a decentralised state system is both feasible and desirable.

Other countries have already moved their seat of government from areas of high-density population to less densely populated areas. Brazil created a new capital in the jungle. In many of the US states, the state capital is not the major business or commercial city. Imagine if our Irish Government had the courage and foresight to start planning now to move the seat of government to the West of Ireland. This would restore balance to the population and reduce the problems created by population agglomeration in and around Dublin.

So who are the advocates of centralisation? The immediate response is to point the finger at the civil service. This is not only facile but unfair. I have had the privilege of meeting very many civil servants, a body of highly professional individuals, and have yet to meet a centraliser.

There is no obvious centraliser, other than the "system" itself. The whole nature of centralism creates a synergy that drives a powerful magnetic force towards a multiplication of the power at the centre. The reason is our inherent reluctance to take responsibility because of a fear of decision-making. The result is increased bureaucracy, increased security for those at the centre, perforce increased state intervention, and an increased reliance on that state intervention. The two largest political parties, Fianna Fáil and Fine Gael, whose guiding principles both seek to reduce state intervention, are oblivious to the fact that they are actively sustaining this paradox. This leads us to blame the politicians. Again, this is an incomplete picture.

The greatest problem is that centralisation of the main organs of the media has created a cosy cartel, with a firm mind-set of centralism. Ably supported by the chief economists as regular columnists, the might of the media is engaged in supporting the pull to the centre. Yet there is no economic proof that, in a land-mass as small as Ireland (and if the policy of equalising the pace of development was adopted), agglomeration is a good economic tool. But what chance has the case for dispersal, local empowerment and decentralisation, when the might of centralised mind-sets, in such influential sectors of our population, is firmly set against it?

The real centralism lies in our mind-set. We all think centrally. We all believe that the only answer to the location of power is at the centre. Ask most county managers for the best location in their county and, without exception, they will think of the county town first. The only person I have ever met who cogently argues the case for reduced centralism is Philip Mullally, Chief Executive of the Enterprise Trust. He passionately believes in the need to reduce centralism to allow people the confidence to take responsibility for their own future. His mission to achieve this goal is no easy one.

The move towards decentralisation should not be confused with a refusal or reluctance of local economies to be involved in the mainstream of global economics. The two are mutually compatible. The local economy must be allowed to develop its own character and the strong, rich cultural personae of its people. This will ultimately lead to the need for a regional development policy to be adopted by Government. Greater local control and greater financial control must once again be legislated for in order to allow real local enterprise to flourish.

Further rationalisation of state services must also be undertaken. Those who might make a contribution to the local enterprise process are confused and feel inadequate and threatened because of the plethora of schemes and programmes that are now in place, bringing a large element of duplication in their wake.

There is plenty of EU and State assistance available for enterprise development. The communications and administrative channels have become totally blocked, rendering access to the system an impossibility except for those who are daily engaged in the process. This has led to a terrible suspicion of bureaucracy and a lack of trust and confidence amongst those who desire to be involved in enterprise.

The state-agency sector continues to be strangled by a top-down decision-making process that has removed large elements of decision-making from the regions. Regional managers of state agencies have been deprived of real autonomy, either administratively or financially. Schemes are decided from the centre. In administering these, regions must endeavour to find people for schemes instead of finding schemes for the real needs of people. The cry for transparency and accountability has given the centralisers their rationale. This need not be so. Transparency and accountability can equally be undertaken in the regions and in local economies with far greater effectiveness and with far less bureaucracy.

The whole process of distributing state funds has lost its effect because of this stranglehold. The distribution of state funds is like throwing popcorn to the ducks in the pond at St Stephen's Green on a windy day. There is little food wasted because other birds pick up the wind-blown food, but the target of feeding the ducks is considerably less effective. So too, the spending of state funds is largely ineffective, because of the massive amount of bureaucracy. The fact that, of the 35 or more state agencies involved in the development process in the country, no two have the same regional boundaries proves the need for rationalisation. The fact that eight Government Departments are now involved in the administration of local enterprise schemes is a further reason why this country is crying out for a policy of regional development and a policy of local development (see Appendix 1). For the same reason, rationalisation of the administration system must occur. I have endeavoured to illustrate these in Appendix 2. I suggest that any lack of clarity reflects less on my graphic abilities and more on the need to simplify the system of schemes, programmes, etc.

That the failed methods of the past must be tackled is obvious to enterprising individuals and community enterprise companies. We must also acknowledge that much of what has been termed enterprise in the past has been little more than a "copy-cat" approach to successful businesses. The lack of innovation and the consequent lack of value-added enterprise has validated the centralisers' cause and their justification for sectoral exclusion clauses in state development schemes on the basis of job displacement. In my opinion, displacement is another one of the mind-sets that needs to be confronted, but this does not lessen the need for us all to be innovative in planning for development.

27

The Next Crossroads

In April 1993, when Fr Harry Bohan told the people of Kiltimagh that they were at a crossroads, he was simply stating a
stark fact that is part of the organic development of community enterprise. One never closes the book on community enterprise.

Kiltimagh is at a crossroads — not the same crossroads as
in 1988 — this one is further up the road — but a crossroads
nonetheless.

For Kiltimagh, the narrow road travelled between 1988 and
1994 began to widen gradually. It continues to widen, making
progress a little easier. The Kiltimagh Team is capable and determined. Joe Kelly, Mary Glynn, Bridie MacMahon, and in the
early years, Claire Cunnane, and I were all learners. None of
us was an expert — we were just a committed team of full-time
professionals who saw our roles more as the vocation of mis-
sionaries than as just a job. We realise that the road ahead is
not built for speed. It requires slow, hard plodding to make
progress towards successful community enterprise.

The voluntary team involved in the process also learned
along the way. The personal development of all team members
through the experience of community development has been
significant.

The team's loyalty to the ongoing development process is
heartening in the extreme. Where else, other than in the ambience of the community spirit that is Kiltimagh, would you find
a regular gathering of committed volunteers congregating in
the front office of Enterprise House almost on a daily basis?
That was generally where the next move was planned or the
next phase of a project tackled.

I recall the comment of one visitor who attended a working
group meeting: "Isn't Kiltimagh lucky to have such profes-

sionals in the voluntary sector?" She was referring in particular to a verbal report given by team member Nancy Lavin, on
efforts to persuade Mayo County Council to build a housing
scheme in the town.

Three features helped to influence public perception:

- The excellent work undertaken by FÁS Employment
Schemes, under the enthusiastic and creative energy of
Chris Glynn. The improvements to the physical infrastruc-
ture and the Heritage Trail are immediately noticeable.

- The refurbishment of the former Continental Hotel into a
modern cosy hotel, aptly named "The Cill Aodáin". A good
hotel in any town is a jewel. The Cill Aodáin has prospered
under the guiding hand of manager Tony McDermott. The
hotel register is emblazoned with the names of German,
French and Dutch visitors enjoying fly-drive holidays. The
attraction of this external investment from the Halligan
family was a great boost to the revival of Kiltimagh.

- The transformation of the Market Square and the townscape generally, undertaken by local businesses in conjunction with Mayo County Council.

These three features have given Kiltimagh the foundation to
attract further indigenous and external investment. It has
challenged the community to take a pro-active role in supporting the development process.

Much has been done. Much more needs to be done. A new
phase of defensive innovation has started. What exists must be
protected. It must also be developed further. The positive innovation phase must also continue, to develop Kiltimagh and to
continue to differentiate it from other towns.

The challenge of continuing the process is enormous. No-one
is more aware of this than the professional staff, the board
members of IRD Kiltimagh and the working groups. All combine to make Kiltimagh a vibrant source of energy. The future
is in good hands.

Conclusion

My successor as General Manager of IRD Kiltimagh, Joe Kelly,
concludes:

The challenge to Kiltimagh is as intense as ever, even if it presents itself in a different guise. The initial gauntlet thrown was one of economic redevelopment of an area decimated by the blight of emigration for almost 50 years.

At that time, however, there existed a deep hunger which, when coupled with the awareness created by the migration study carried out by Fr Brennan in 1988 and by a subsequent series of articles in *The Irish Times*, mobilised the community spirit for which Kiltimagh has become renowned over many years.

Seven years after the initial study, some relative successes have been attained. The facilitation of the creation of over 200 jobs in the East Mayo area is no mean achievement and was not even considered in the wildest aspirations of the initial group that carried out the early planning phase of IRD Kiltimagh. Couple this with the increase in economic activities, the increase in property prices and the economic redevelopment programme, and Kiltimagh can surely count its successes. Much has been achieved in the area of village enhancement and community development. Social development is now receiving a major push. These relative successes have led to a change in the challenge. The challenge now is to sustain the projects that have been put in place and the impetus achieved to date.

The threat to these is very real and could become a cancer on the very heart of community enterprise — not only in Kiltimagh, but throughout Ireland and, to a degree, internationally. If Kiltimagh fails, having been hailed as a flagship of redevelopment and the bottom-up approach, it will lead to despair among other communities, many of whom are just beginning their own local process. Even those individuals who escape the despair will be greeted by cries of "Sure, they tried that in Kiltimagh and see what happened", when they try to mobilise their own communities or fund-raise locally.

The reason why this threat is so real in Kiltimagh almost six years after the inception of IRD Kiltimagh is that, although the community spirit continues unabated (as evidenced by the continuing numbers of people involved voluntarily on behalf of the company), the hunger that existed in 1988 no longer carries the same pang or urgency. In addition, many people have "great expectations" that the impetus will be maintained, though they feel themselves that they "have done their bit".

Unfortunately, "eaten bread is soon forgotten", and Kiltimagh of the 1980s with its derelict appearance is as dim a memory as the last World War. The local community needs to realise that the work can only continue with its help, in terms of voluntary commitment and subscriptions to the projects undertaken by the company.

It is a fact also that, after six years of success on a shoe-string budget that has produced favourable results, our successive Governments have failed to make any provision for the direct funding of the local development process needed to bring projects to fruition. If all monies raised among the local community must be used to sustain an administrative structure, where do the matching funds for grants towards projects (which are readily available) come from?

However, all is not doom and gloom. Any community intent on effective development must take a pro-active role and work to a pre-agreed plan, based on the needs of the people, coupled with the resources of the area. Kiltimagh is no different. A plan was prepared in 1990 and executed between then and 1994. A new plan has been developed, involving the same approach as before — a large number of projects rather than a single large project. The flagship project will be the establishment of a School of Music for the North West — as ambitious in its outlook as the provision of Enterprise Units in the first phase of planning.

Like any other community, we have looked to the resources of the area and have developed projects in agriculture, tourism, cultural heritage, etc. Most of these projects are being vigorously pursued by our many working groups. Projects such as the enhancement of the area are set to continue under the theme of "Kiltimagh — the Bilingual Artisan Village", in conjunction with Bord na Gaeilge. Tá áthas mór orainn bheith ag obair le Bord na Gaeilge agus úsáid a bhaint as ár cultúir agus ár teanga gach lá i gCoillte Mach.

The company needs to reduce its reliance on the local community, the state agencies and Local Authorities, all of whom have gone beyond the call of duty over the past six years to fund administration. To this end, the company has taken steps to develop projects that will yield an income. Most of these are in the incubation stage. One that is well-advanced is RIMS, a computerised Reservation and Information Marketing System, created by WDN Limited, Galway and IRD Kiltimagh Limited.

IRD Kiltimagh will be administering the LEADER II and Local Development Programmes in East Mayo. It is imperative that the company does not become just a grant dispenser/programme administrator, as would be so easy, given that these programmes are guaranteed to be self-sustaining. However, they do not necessarily result in effective community development or animation.

In conclusion, the years ahead will be no different for IRD Kiltimagh than for any other development group. They will be marked by crests and troughs, disappointments and ecstasy (the non-oral type!), successes and failures. It is to be hoped that, as before, the good features will far outweigh the negative and, at the turn of the millennium, we will all see a Kiltimagh very different from the Kiltimagh of 1995 and unrecognisable from the Kiltimagh of the late 1980s.

Given the level of commitment of the Chairman, Brian Mooney, and the other members of the board of directors, the working groups and indeed my own staff in the office, I have no doubt but that, bit by bit, project by project, our plan will come to fruition, complemented by the efforts of our friends in the state agencies and Local Authorities whose involvement is central and crucial to the development process.

Ar aghaidh 2000 le chéile.

Joe Kelly
General Manager

Appendix 1:

EU and State Schemes for Development

Many people are perplexed by the plethora of state schemes and programmes available to assist development. This Appendix attempts to show:

- The Process of Government Planning for EU Support
- State and EU Schemes by Initiative
- State and EU Schemes by Government Department.

If it all seems somewhat complicated, that's because it is!

The Process of Government Planning for EU Support

The Government has set out its development plans in a series of documents, depicted below:

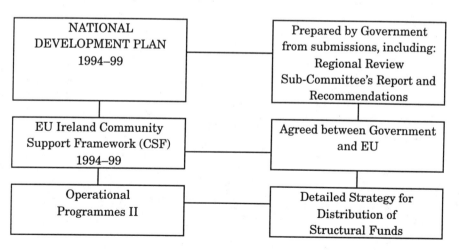

NATIONAL DEVELOPMENT PLAN 1994–99	Prepared by Government from submissions, including: Regional Review Sub-Committee's Report and Recommendations
EU Ireland Community Support Framework (CSF) 1994–99	Agreed between Government and EU
Operational Programmes II	Detailed Strategy for Distribution of Structural Funds

The main areas of focus in this planning process are:

1.   Local, Urban and Rural Development

2.   Tourism

3.   Industry

4.   Human Resources

5.   Transport

6.   Environment

7.   Agriculture, Rural Development and Forestry

8.   Fisheries

9.   Energy

10. Communications

11. Border Regions.

State and EU Schemes by Initiative

Under the first round of Structural Funds, the EU operated a series of 13 Community Initiatives. These were global grants given to community groups and other local development agents (in some cases, third-level colleges) to administer. They were monitored by the relevant Government Departments.

These initiatives have been amended and revised for the second round of Structural Funds. Some of the revised programmes are relevant to community groups and local development agents and some of those commenced already are shown below.

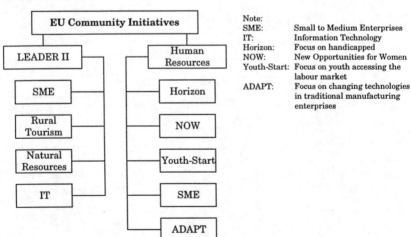

Note:
SME: Small to Medium Enterprises
IT: Information Technology
Horizon: Focus on handicapped
NOW: New Opportunities for Women
Youth-Start: Focus on youth accessing the labour market
ADAPT: Focus on changing technologies in traditional manufacturing enterprises

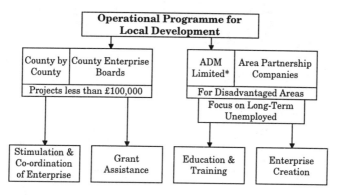

* Area Development Management Limited: Established to administer the Area Partnership Companies from offices in Dublin

Most of the Operational Programmes are relevant only to Local Authorities and state or semi-state bodies. The exceptions are larger development projects involving investments in excess of £100,000.

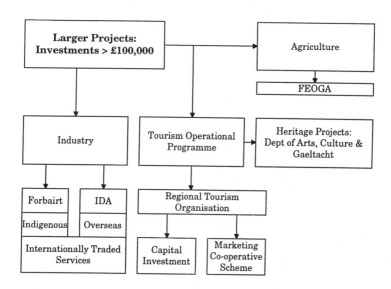

State and EU Schemes by Government Department

On a Department by Department basis, the distribution of local Enterprise Schemes can be depicted as follows:

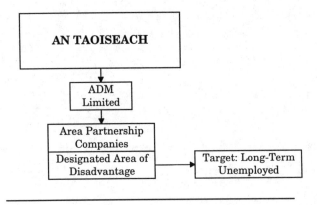

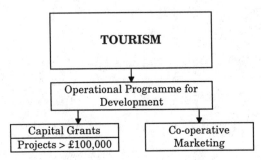

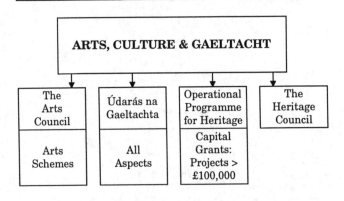

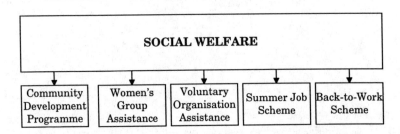

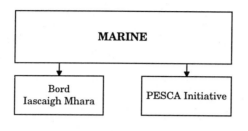

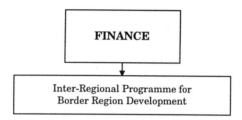

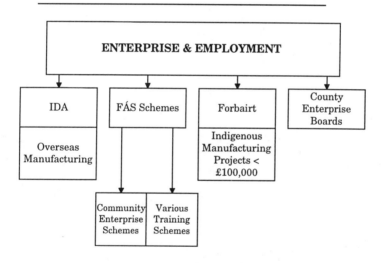

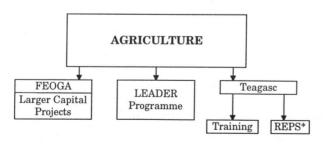

*   Rural Environmental Protection Scheme

Appendix 2:

The Which, What, Who and How Guide for Community Development Organisations

Which Scheme?	What For?	Who Administers?	How to Apply	Subject to Closing Date?
ADAPT	Adapting to Changing Technology	Department of Enterprise and Employment, via Local Groups	Application Form and Workplan	Yes
Arts Development	Operational Aspects of Arts Development	The Arts Council	Plan/Report	Generally February each Year
Back-to-Work Scheme	Unemployed Returning to Work	Department of Social Welfare (Regional Offices)	Application Form	No
Community Development Programme	Social Development Programmes	Department of Social Welfare (Regional Offices)	Workplan	No
FÁS	Employment and Training Schemes	FÁS Regional Offices	Application Form	No
FEOGA	Large Food-Development Projects	Forbairt and Department of Agriculture	Application Form and Business Plan	No

Which Scheme?	What For?	Who Administers?	How to Apply	Subject to Closing Date?
Forbairt	Indigenous Manufacturing Projects	Forbairt Regional Offices	Business Plan	No
Horizon	Development Programme for Handicapped/ Disabled	Department of Enterprise and Employ- ment, via Local Groups	Application Form and Workplan	Yes
INTERREG	Border Region Development	Department of Finance, via Local Groups	Workplan	Yes
LEADER	Community or Individual Enterprises	LEADER Company (Local Development Companies)	Application Form/ Other Plans/ Reports	No
NOW	Development Programmes for Women's Groups	Department of Enterprise and Employ- ment, via Local Groups	Application Form and Workplan	Yes
Operational Programme for Local Development	Business Development	County Enterprise Board (County by County)	Report or Business Plan	No
Operational Programme for Local Development	Training/ Enterprise for Unemployed	Area Partnership Company (Local Area)	Direct contact with local APC Office	No
Operational Programme for Tourism	Tourism Development or Marketing	Regional Tourism Offices	Application Form and Business Plan	Yes
Operational Programme for Tourism	Heritage Projects	Department of Arts, Culture and Gaeltacht	Application Form and Business Plan	Yes

Which Scheme?	What For?	Who Administers?	How to Apply	Subject to Closing Date?
PESCA	Local Fisheries Development	Department of the Marine	Business Plan/ Workplan	Yes
Rural Environmental Protection Scheme	On-Farm Environmental Protection	Teagasc (County by County)	Workplan	No
SMEs	Development of Small Enterprises for Networking	Department of Enterprise and Employment, via Forbairt	Application Form and Workplan	Yes
Summer Jobs Scheme	Students' Summer Scheme	Department of Social Welfare (Regional Offices)	Application Form	Spring each Year
URBAN	Development of Urban Enterprises	Local Development Companies, via Local Groups	Business Plan	Yes
Voluntary Organisation Schemes	Development Programmes (once-off)	Department of Social Welfare (Regional Offices)	Workplan	No
Women's Groups	Development Programmes (once-off)	Department of Social Welfare (Regional Offices)	Workplan	No
Youth-Start	Development Programme for Youth Entering Workplace	Department of Enterprise and Employment, via Local Groups	Application Form and Workplan	Yes